By Man Least
Understood

By Man Least
Understood

By
Derek G. Rowley

CFI
Springville, Utah

ISBN: 978–1–55517–940–3

Published by CFI, an imprint of Cedar Fort, Inc., 2373 W. 700 S., Springville, UT, 84663
Distributed by Cedar Fort, Inc. www.cedarfort.com

Library of Congress Cataloging-in-Publication Data

    Rowley, Derek G.
      By man least understood : repentance, agency, restoration, atonement, and the everlasting covenant / Derek G. Rowley.
        p. cm.
    Includes bibliographical references and index.
    ISBN 978–1–55517–940–3 (alk. paper)
    1. Jesus Christ—Mormon interpretations. 2. Atonement. 3. Church of Jesus Christ of Latter day Saints—Doctrines. 4. Mormon Church—Doctrines. I. Title.

    BX8643.J4R69 2007
    234—dc22

                             2007004797

Cover design by Nicole Williams
Cover design © 2007 by Lyle Mortimer
Edited and typeset by Erin L. Cameron

Printed in the United States of America

10 9 8 7 6 5 4 3 2 1

Printed on acid-free paper

Contents

Acknowledgments

THIS BOOK IS THE RESULT OF MANY HOURS of study, pondering, and gospel discussion with family, Church leaders, and others whose opinions I value. While my name ultimately appears as the author, this work would not have been possible without the assistance and support of many people. Foremost, I am grateful to and for my eternal companion, Genine, who has unfailingly supported my efforts. I have been unable to pull from her a single criticism of anything I've written in any of the earlier drafts because, as she always tells me, "You know I love everything you do." How great is that?

Thanks also to many others: President William Brewer of the Carson City Nevada Stake for sacrificing his time to provide me with his suggestions and insights; my long-time friend Brian Foote for our extended, long-distance discussions on the topics herein and for the valuable input and direction he provided; and my father, Vernon C. Rowley, for his technical suggestions and proofreading efforts. I am also grateful to Lee Nelson at Cedar Fort for working with me to publish this book.

I ought to thank many others who have contributed to my testimony and religious experiences over the years, but they are too numerous to name here. I hope you know who you are, and I hope that I've taken the opportunity to thank you personally.

Introduction

CHURCH LEADERS AND SCHOLARS HAVE WRITTEN MUCH IN recent years about the Atonement. It is central to God's plan of happiness for His children. I believe this with all of my being. Modern apostles—special witnesses of the Savior—have testified and written a great deal on the implications of the Atonement in our lives. These teachings have greatly blessed us all.

Some active Church members—despite the clear teachings of prophets and apostles—believe that the Atonement of Jesus Christ has merely a theoretical application in their lives. Many of us partake of the sacrament with only a cursory understanding of it. We may also have listened to—or even taught—lessons related to the Atonement in which we've felt no real, personal connection with it. For many of us, the discussion of the Atonement is more academic than doctrinal. As I felt prompted to begin writing, I became aware of a need to take a Christ- and covenant-centered approach to some familiar doctrine from a different perspective. I believe the purpose for doing this has been to strengthen my own testimony and to increase my own understanding of the many direct implications of Christ's atoning sacrifice in my own life. If anything in this book helps you in strengthening your testimony of the Savior, so much the better.

All elements of the gospel of Jesus Christ—each of the revealed commandments, ordinances, covenants, blessings, miracles, and promises—

relate directly to the atoning sacrifice of our Savior. The Atonement encompasses everything. Christ entered into a premortal covenant that was necessary to bring to pass man's salvation; without this covenant, everything would cease to exist.

It is by Him and through Him that the heavens and the earth were created, and it was because of Him that there was a reason for the heavens and the earth to exist. The heavens exist that the world might have a place to reside. The world exists that man might be and have joy. Bringing to pass man's eternal life and exaltation is the very work and glory of God (see Moses 1:39). The Savior's obedience, sacrifice, love, power, and purity allowed the Father's plan to proceed, so Christ could declare:

> I am Alpha and Omega, Christ the Lord; yea, even I am he, the beginning and the end, the Redeemer of the world.
>
> I, having accomplished and finished the will of him whose I am, even the Father, concerning me—having done this that I might subdue all things unto myself—
>
> Retaining all power, even to the destroying of Satan and his works at the end of the world, and the last great day of judgment, which I shall pass upon the inhabitants thereof, judging every man according to his works and the deeds which he hath done. (D&C 19:1–3)

To us, Jesus Christ truly is the beginning and the end of all things. Not only is there "none other name given under heaven save it be this Jesus Christ, of which I have spoken, whereby man can be saved" (2 Nephi 25:20), but also there is no other name under heaven whereby man can be blessed, forgiven, anointed, sanctified, sealed, healed, perfected, ordained, endowed, and exalted.

He has given unto us His gospel, which, in His own words, is "that I came into the world to do the will of my Father, because my Father sent me" (3 Nephi 27:13). This incredible statement by the "messenger of salvation" (D&C 93:8) boils down an endless and eternal plan into exquisite simplicity. This statement succinctly encompasses all the breadths and depths of revealed doctrine. Christ came to fulfill the law and the prophets (Matthew 5:17).

Such a condensed and simplistic description of the gospel may seem beyond the grasp of the natural man, so we are not expected to understand it all at once. After a lifetime of regular, prayerful study, having received "line upon line, precept upon precept" (D&C 98:12) we may only begin to understand the significance of Christ having done the will of the Father simply because the Father had sent Him, and what that understanding requires of us. As we live the principles we learn, the scriptures promise that we will become "full of charity towards all men, and to the household of faith," and we will "let virtue garnish [our] thoughts unceasingly; then shall [our] confidence wax strong in the presence of God; and the doctrine of the priesthood shall distil upon [our] soul as the dews from heaven" (D&C 121:45).

The title *By Man Least Understood* comes from a line in one of my favorite sacrament hymns of the restored Church, "O God, the Eternal Father," written by William W. Phelps. I chose to use this phrase as the title of this book as it is used in the context of the hymn. I am not attempting to explain—nor do I believe that I am capable of explaining—the "least understood" doctrine of the gospel. I selected this phrase to acknowledge that there is much that we do not understand about Christ's atoning sacrifice and that it is woven throughout the tapestry of gospel principles, covenants, and doctrine.

O God, th' Eternal Father,
Who dwells amid the sky,
In Jesus' name we ask thee
To bless and sanctify,
If we are pure before thee,
This bread and cup of wine,
That we may all remember
That offering divine—

That sacred, holy off'ring,
By man least understood,
To have our sins remitted
And take his flesh and blood,
That we may ever witness
The suff'ring of thy Son,
And always have his spirit
To make our hearts as one.

When Jesus, the Anointed,
Descended from above
And gave himself a ransom
To win our souls with love—
With no apparent beauty,

That man should him desire—
He was the promised Savior,
To purify with fire.

How infinite that wisdom,
The plan of holiness,
That made salvation perfect
And veiled the Lord in flesh,
To walk upon his footstool
And be like man, almost,
In his exalted station,
And die, or all was lost.[1]

I want to discuss a few select doctrinal principles in light of two realities: the Atonement is central to the gospel, and it is a doctrine "least understood." This concept can be compared to the scientific principle of gravity. Gravity is, in one sense, known; its consequences are sure and calculable. We know gravity exists and see it working all around us, yet scientists still do not completely understand it. Or consider the phenomenon of light. Is there anything so ubiquitous, yet so little understood, as light? Scientists have conducted tests that support the theories that light is transmitted as a wave of energy and also, contradictorily, as a particle of matter. For all that is known about light and its properties, we still do not have a firm grasp on it. The same is true of the Atonement.

Starting with the basic principle of repentance, this book discusses the restoration of priesthood keys and ordinances, gospel covenants, and personal restoration in the context of the everlasting covenant. Repentance is the process by which the power of the Atonement and the guidance of the gift of the Holy Ghost ultimately become available to us, so repentance is the thread that ties all these principles together throughout these chapters. Repentance allows us to receive the gifts, blessings, and miracles that result from the covenant which Christ entered into before the worlds were created.

Perhaps the greatest of all of God's miracles is found when the sincerely penitent forever change their hearts. President Spencer W. Kimball

---

1. "O God, the Eternal Father," *Hymns of The Church of Jesus Christ of Latter-day Saints*, (Salt Lake City: The Church of Jesus Christ of Latter-day Saints, 1985) 175.

identified the sacred rarity of this process in the title of his book, *The Miracle of Forgiveness*. Forgiveness is indeed a miracle, brought about only because of the selfless sacrifice of our Savior. It is a miracle because it is only through the enabling power of God's grace that we can achieve exaltation in our temporal, fallen, and sinful state. There is nothing we can do to grant ourselves God's forgiveness. The Atonement makes something of us that is far beyond our own capacities.

In *The Broken Heart*, Elder Bruce C. Hafen taught: "Through the miracle of the Atonement and through the grace and power of the Savior, this means that—if our repentance is complete—he will compensate for our failures, our sins, and our mistakes. It further means that he will perfect us—make us truly excellent—beyond our power to perfect ourselves."[2]

Forgiveness is a miraculous gift. It is the perfect, ultimate gift, given to us by the ultimate sacrifice of the perfect Savior, Jesus Christ. It is a gift that we are able to receive by our faith and diligence and through our repentance. We have no inherent right—by our own mortal strength alone—to claim the gifts available to us through the Atonement, which is where the marvelous concept of grace begins to apply in our lives. The Lord has clearly spoken to us through His prophets, saying, "I, the Lord, will forgive whom I will forgive" (D&C 64:10). He has, however, given us a promise that those who follow Him, have faith in His name, and repent of their sins will receive this great miracle of forgiveness. "Behold, he sendeth an invitation unto all men, for the arms of mercy are extended towards them, and he saith: *Repent, and I will receive you*" (Alma 5:33, emphasis added).

I have always felt that one of our struggles as members of the restored Church is that we understand our relationship with the Savior in different terms than our friends of other Christian faiths. Many of them speak confidently of having been "saved," while we avoid making such a personal claim; we feel it is not for us to judge, and our understanding of Christ's sacrifice tells us that being "saved" is a lifelong process—rather than a single event—that involves continual obedience to covenants, ordinances, and commandments. Our understanding of Jesus Christ as the literal Son of God is a difficult doctrine to Christians who accept the mysterious, negotiated creeds of fourth-

---

2. Hafen, Bruce C. *The Broken Heart: Applying the Atonement to Life's Experiences* (Salt Lake City, Utah: Deseret Book, 1989).

century committees. We may feel that those creeds have left much of the Christian world with a God that is difficult to define and nearly impossible to understand. Critics of the Church use these differences against us and portray Latter-day Saints as non-Christian and sometimes even anti-Christian.

Our understanding and application of gospel covenants is significant in our faith and sets us apart from other Christians. Perhaps if we had a stronger, more intimate witness and understanding of not only the personal role of Christ's Atonement in our lives but also the manner and degree in which all gospel covenants and doctrine are reliant upon it, we would be less susceptible to such outside criticism.

The doctrine and mission of the Church encompass such far-reaching principles as commandments, revelation, family history work, food storage, worship meetings, employment, Scouting, temple work, humanitarian aid, missionary work, education, cultural events, and Church auxiliaries. "Cultural doctrine" also exists in some parts of the kingdom; many of us are caught up in BYU athletics, compete over the "quality" of our Church callings, or boast about our pioneer lineage. These activities may distract us to the point that we fail to remember that it is the Savior's sacrifice that makes all good things possible for us.

It is difficult to address the fundamental principles of repentance and forgiveness in a way that helps the average Church member bring about meaningful change. I do not know if I have helped people change, but the principles in this book have made a difference in my own life.

Much of this book is a detailed account of my testimony. My testimony of the Savior has come to me quietly but firmly as I have experienced the power of repentance in my own life and have counseled others. What I know of the reality of Christ—of the personal, yet infinite nature of His sacrifice and of the priesthood keys that provide access to His atoning powers—I know only because I have felt His forgiveness and have heard the still, small voice. I have gained a better understanding of certain scriptures and principles. I hope that some of the insights that have blessed my life with greater appreciation for the Savior may also bless someone else's.

I have seen many struggle under the weight of repentance and have watched as mighty miracles occurred in the lives of individuals and families as a result. I need to continually practice repentance as well, though I do it imperfectly. The greatest lessons that I have been taught about repentance have been by the whisperings of the Holy Ghost during the process, as the Lord saw fit.

Because of my own personal experiences with repentance and how I have seen it in the lives of others, I have come to believe that one of the divine purposes that repentance serves is to give each of us an opportunity to gain our own personal witness of the reality of the Atonement of Jesus Christ. A testimony that is founded upon that revelation, resulting from repentance, is like the house built upon the rock. Combine that type of testimony with a clear understanding of our covenants, blessings, and doctrine, and there exists great power to accomplish whatsoever our Father in Heaven will require of us. There has been a lot of talk in the Church recently about "raising the bar." The bar for current and future full-time missionaries needs to be raised, as President Gordon B. Hinckley has said. This may come as the consequence of families being raised with the type of testimonies and knowledge that come from repentance.

We still have a great work to do, individually and collectively. May we be diligent in our repentance and in our efforts to gain the light and knowledge we will need to protect ourselves and our families, that we may survive Satan's onslaught in these last days. May we look only to the Savior, that we might receive the blessings of eternal life and be saved in His kingdom.

I make no attempt to speak for The Church of Jesus Christ of Latter-day Saints. This book is not, by any means, official Church doctrine. The only credential I bring to this work is a desire, as Alma wrote, that perhaps I may have a role in the hands of God "to bring some soul to repentance; and this is my joy" (Alma 29:9).

I take full responsibility for the contents of this book, which is not intended as a definitive work on any of the gospel principles discussed herein. On the topics of repentance and forgiveness, President Kimball's inspired book continues to remain the standard work and is highly recommended to anyone in need of greater insight into these principles.

—Derek G. Rowley

CHAPTER ONE

The Fruit of Repentance

> And now, my brethren, I would that ye should humble yourselves
> before God, and bring forth fruit meet for repentance, that ye may
> also enter into that rest.
>
> —*Alma 13:13*

FAITH IS PREREQUISITE TO REPENTANCE, AND ANY IN-DEPTH discussion
of the principle of faith eventually invokes the concepts of vision and
sight. For example, Paul, in his epistle to the Hebrews, wrote that "faith
is the substance of things hoped for, the evidence of things not seen,"
and that through faith we can understand that "things which are seen
were not made of things which do appear" (Hebrews 11:1, 3). Paul tells
us that having faith gives us more than just our natural senses to see
things of eternity. Through faith, we can actually see and know things
that are otherwise "not seen." Paul goes on in that epistle to recount
that the prophets—Abel, Enoch, Noah, Abraham, and others—were
able to fulfill their callings only after having obtained the vision of
their callings by faith. Increasing our faith in Christ expands both the
depth and scope of our eternal vision.

Joseph Smith taught that it is the "substance of things hoped for"
that motivates our every action and influences our every choice:

> Would you have ever sown, if you had not believed that you
> would reap? Would you have ever planted, if you had not believed
> that you would gather? Would you have ever asked, unless you had
> believed that you would receive? Would you have ever sought unless
> you had believed that you would have found? Or, would you have
> ever knocked, unless you had believed that it would have been open
> unto you? In a word, is there anything that you would have done,

either physical or mental, if you had not previously believed? Are not all your exertions of every kind, dependent on your faith? Or may we not ask, what have you, or what do you possess, which you have not obtained by reason of your faith? Your food, your raiment, your lodgings, are they not all by reason of your faith? Reflect, and ask yourselves if these things are not so.[1]

Laman and Lemuel derisively called their father, Lehi, a visionary man when he led his family out of Jerusalem into the wilderness, leaving their riches—and the world as they knew it—behind (1 Nephi 2:11). It was a fitting title, however, for their father had "written many things which he saw in visions and in dreams" (1 Nephi 1:16). In the very moment of their mocking and sarcasm, Laman and Lemuel were actually testifying and acknowledging that their father was a man of great faith. He had received assurance of things hoped for and had obtained significant evidence of things not seen with his natural eyes. Lehi had seen, through the visionary eyes of faith, the fate of not only his immediate family, but also his entire posterity. Through faith, he had seen the end from the beginning.

In our own personal journeys through repentance, we cannot see the end from the beginning without exercising and expanding our faith. Obtaining evidence of things not seen can be quite a challenge, but faith—eternal vision—will lead us directly to repentance. The more we see of the blessings of the great plan of redemption and of the Atonement, the more we will desire to set our sins aside and follow the Savior. That is when we make the choice to come unto Him.

Many who are entangled in the web of sin struggle with the reality that they cannot use their temporal senses to see, touch, and taste the fruit of repentance. They feel that they cannot gain an intimate understanding of the gospel and its blessings because they are intangible. In Lehi's vision of the Tree of Life, Lehi described the fruit of the tree—symbolic of the fruit of the gospel—as being "desirable to make one happy" and "most sweet, above all that I ever before tasted." Lehi then continued, "And as I partook of the fruit thereof it filled my soul with exceedingly great joy; wherefore, I began to be desirous that my family should partake of it also; for I knew that it was desirable above all other fruit" (1 Nephi 8:10–12).

----

1.   Joseph Smith, *Lectures on Faith*, (Salt Lake City: Deseret Book, 1985) 2–3

As Lehi taught his family about the great joy that the fruit brought to his soul, they had to rely on his words until they could experience the taste of the fruit themselves. Lehi's words were sufficient evidence for some, but not all of his family shared his eternal vision. Laman and Lemuel lacked the faith and vision to see what Lehi saw; however, Nephi's great faith in his father's words—and his great desire to experience what his father had experienced—led him to receive the same vision. His eye was single to the glory of God, and with the prize in view, he was willing to do what was necessary to obtain it.

When we can see the fruit of repentance in our lives, the prize becomes attainable, and we can obtain it. It becomes our "substance of things hoped for." We will then be able to feel it, smell it, and ultimately taste it, as Lehi did. If we hunger for this fruit in our lives and if we earnestly seek it, the Lord will bless us with the faith that will allow us to partake. So, we will begin by looking toward the end: the fruit of repentance.

IDENTIFYING IMMEDIATE IMPACTS

> Beware of false prophets, which come to you in sheep's clothing, but inwardly they are ravening wolves.
>
> Ye shall know them by their fruits. Do men gather grapes of thorns, or figs of thistles?
>
> Even so every good tree bringeth forth good fruit; but a corrupt tree bringeth forth evil fruit.
>
> A good tree cannot bring forth evil fruit, neither can a corrupt tree bring forth good fruit.
>
> Every tree that bringeth not forth good fruit is hewn down, and cast into the fire.
>
> Wherefore by their fruits ye shall know them. (Matthew 7:15–20)

Repentance bears significant, life-changing fruit. The value of repentance is found not only in the promises of the eternities but also in the blessings of today and tomorrow. Repentance changes us in a real and practical way. By letting go of our burdens of sin, we become free. Elements of our agency are restored to us as we turn away from compulsive and habit-forming sin. Of this principle, Leo Tolstoy has been attributed to have said, "He who understands [Christ's teachings], feels like a bird who did not know it had wings, and suddenly realizes that it can fly; it can be free; and no longer needs to fear."

As a young missionary, I was called to teach the gospel of repentance in Singapore and Malaysia. I taught a thirty-something-year-old man named Desmond. Desmond had immersed himself in the competitive culture of materialism and worldly acquisition that defined the economic engine of Singapore at that time. At a relatively young age, he had become unusually successful. He drove an exotic car, while most people in his area used public transportation. Unmarried, he lived alone in a condominium, which he owned, in a time when it was common for families to live together with several generations occupying cramped, public housing flats.

He was educated in the things of the world, yet he had the wisdom to recognize that he was profoundly unhappy despite his possessions and accomplishments. He told me that he felt he was experiencing no joy in his materialistic pursuit and that he was trapped by a lifestyle that was clearly not in harmony with God's commandments.

After much study and prayer, Desmond discovered the power of the gospel of Jesus Christ. He learned of the principle of repentance and how it could bring purpose and value to his life. He was freed from the trappings of sin that bound him. His wealth turned from a burden to a great blessing. Meaning was restored to his life when he entered into the sacred covenants that began in the waters of baptism. He experienced the joy that emanates from the covenant to always have "His Spirit to be with [him]" (D&C 20:77, 79). Desmond became like Tolstoy's bird; he acted as if he suddenly realized his spiritual potential and learned to use it. He did not hope for some vague, remote time for the gospel to bless him for his faith to make it all worthwhile. He immediately saw the blessings of repentance, and they touched every aspect of his spiritual and temporal being. His experience is not unique.

Repentance has not only a direct, positive spiritual impact, but also positive physiological and psychological influences as well. I have seen many people consumed by the consciousness of their guilt. Like Alma the Younger, they were "racked with the pains of a damned soul," "in the gall of bitterness," "encircled about by the everlasting chains of death," and "harrowed up by the memory of [their] many sins" (Alma 36:16–18). Repentance influences the soul, emotionally and physically. It can change a person's entire outlook on life and can be the answer to many of today's health concerns. It may assist in relieving depression, which is epidemic in our society; it may contribute to a more restful sleep; it may relieve stress and anxiety; it may lower blood pressure over time; and it may even help overcome secondary health disorders and compulsions.

It is important for everyone involved in the repentance process to understand and to be able to identify the fruits of repentance. The repentant need to be able to see and identify when their repentance bears worthy fruit. Priesthood leaders eagerly look for the fruits of repentance in the lives of those they counsel. Missionaries should look for the fruit of repentance in potential converts' lives if they want to inspire true conversion and baptism.

While in the wilderness of Judea, John the Baptist addressed the Pharisees, the Sadducees, and a multitude who had come to be baptized. He taught:

> O generation of vipers, who hath warned you to flee from the wrath to come?
>
> Bring forth therefore fruits worthy of repentance, and begin not to say within yourselves, We have Abraham to our father: for I say unto you, That God is able of these stones to raise up children unto Abraham.
>
> And now also the axe is laid unto the root of the trees: *every tree therefore which bringeth not forth good fruit is hewn down, and cast into the fire.* (Luke 3:7–9, emphasis added)

John admonished the multitude that unless they changed their lives and brought forth "worthy fruit," their claim to the blessings of Abraham through lineage had no value. He warned them in clear language that without bringing forth good fruit, there would be no place for them in the kingdom of God.

It is still our responsibility today to bear good fruit. Like in ancient times, we will be blessed when we bear the fruit of humility, righteous desires, heeding promptings from the Spirit, and forgiving others. Only then are we worthy to experience true repentance.

HUMILITY

Alma the Younger, speaking to a group of apostate priesthood holders in the land of Ammonihah, taught an important principle. He explains that high priests are called and ordained as the result of their "exceeding faith and repentance" (Alma 13:10) and are "sanctified by the Holy

Ghost, having their garments made white, being pure and spotless before God" (Alma 13:12). He then tells them:

> And now, my brethren, I would that ye should *humble yourselves before God, and bring forth fruit meet for repentance,* that ye may also enter into that rest.
>
> Yea, *humble yourselves* even as the people in the days of Melchizedek, who was also a high priest after this same order which I have spoken, who also took upon him the high priesthood forever. (Alma 13:13–14, emphasis added)

Alma suggests that bringing forth the fruit of repentance is an ongoing responsibility. Even those who have already been sanctified by the Holy Ghost need to bear this fruit. Perhaps the pure and spotless have a greater responsibility to show this fruit than others. Alma then gives additional instruction for bearing the fruit:

> Yea, humble yourselves even as the people in the days of Melchizedek. (Alma 13:14)

> But that ye would humble yourselves before the Lord, and call on his holy name, and watch and pray continually, that ye may not be tempted above that which ye can bear, and thus be led by the Holy Spirit, *becoming humble, meek, submissive, patient, full of love and all long-suffering;*
>
> Having faith on the Lord; having a hope that ye shall receive eternal life; having the love of God always in your hearts, that ye may be lifted up at the last day and enter into his rest. (Alma 13:28–29, emphasis added)

Alma picks some of the sweetest fruit to place before his brethren: he mentions faith, hope, charity, meekness, long-suffering, prayer, patience, and humility. Each of these attributes is worthy of an entire book; in fact, entire books have been written about each of them. Humility, however, is mentioned by Alma not only first but also three separate times, emphasizing its importance as a primary "worthy fruit."

Alma knows from firsthand experience that repentance leaves people humble. Humility is one fruit of true repentance that always blossoms. He described to his son Helaman his feelings of inadequacy and humility that resulted from his introductory experience with repentance in his testimony:

The very thought of coming into the presence of my God did rack my soul with inexpressible horror.

Oh, thought I, that I could be banished and become extinct both soul and body, that I might not be brought to stand in the presence of my God, to be judged of my deeds. (Alma 36:13–16)

Alma was qualified to speak of humility. He knew that humility is purer, more blessed, and more acceptable to the Lord if it comes willingly, naturally, and voluntarily, instead of—as was his experience—being thrust upon him by circumstances. Later, having been rejected by the priests and their community among the Zoramites, Alma taught a multitude on the hill Onidah:

And now, because ye are compelled to be humble blessed are ye; for a man sometimes, if he is compelled to be humble, seeketh repentance; and now surely, whosoever repenteth shall find mercy; and he that findeth mercy and endureth to the end the same shall be saved.

And now, as I said unto you, that because ye were compelled to be humble ye were blessed, do ye not suppose that they are more blessed who truly humble *themselves* because of the word?

Yea, he that truly humbleth himself, and repenteth of his sins, and endureth to the end, the same shall be blessed—yea, much more blessed than they who are compelled to be humble because of their exceeding poverty.

Therefore, blessed are they *who humble themselves without being compelled to be humble.* (Alma 32:13–16, emphasis added)

Humility is the primary fruit of repentance. It blooms very early in the season of repentance. Through the repentance process, the proud and the hard-hearted become meek, submissive, and teachable. King Benjamin taught that humility is essential to the process of repentance because it is only through the "depths of humility" that a remission of sins is retained:

And again I say unto you as I have said before, that as ye have come to the knowledge of the glory of God, or if ye have known of his goodness and have tasted of his love, and have received a remission of your sins, which causeth such exceedingly great joy in your souls, even so *I would that ye should remember, and always retain in your remembrance, the greatness of God, and your own nothingness,* and his goodness and long-suffering towards you, unworthy creatures, and *humble yourselves even in the depths of humility,* calling on the name of the Lord daily, and standing steadfastly in the faith of that which is to come, which was spoken by the mouth of the angel.

And behold, I say unto you that *if ye do this* ye shall always rejoice, and be filled with the love of God, *and always retain a remission of your sins;* and ye shall grow in the knowledge of the glory of him that created you, or in the knowledge of that which is just and true. (Mosiah 4:11–12, emphasis added)

It is a great promise that as we humble ourselves, we will always rejoice and will never have reason to doubt whether God loves us, for we will be filled with His love. And, thus filled, we may truly come to know Him.

MAINTAINING RIGHTEOUS DESIRES

"If he hath repented of his sins, and desired righteousness until the end of his days, even so he shall be rewarded unto righteousness" (Alma 41:6). The Savior's penetrating inquiry, "What desirest thou?" (D&C 7:1) demands significant self-introspection. Ultimately, we are only the sum of our desires. Our actions are rooted in our desires, and our desires come from the thoughts we entertain. When the Lord asks, "What desirest thou?" it is as if He is asking us to answer "Who are you, really?" Repentance changes who we really are at our core, so at the end of the repentance process, we emerge with new desires.

Perhaps this is what Alma means when he speaks of a "change of heart" (Alma 5:14). When the Savior taught that "blessed are the pure in heart: for they shall see God" (Matthew 5:8), He was also referencing this mighty change.

One of the steps to repentance—discussed later in greater detail—requires the repentant to forsake sinful behavior. We must desire to keep all the commandments of the Lord. This too is a significant fruit. Joseph Smith delivered valuable instruction for this dispensation: "Nevertheless, he that repents and does the commandments of the Lord shall be forgiven" (D&C 1:32).

As I have guided priesthood holders through the repentance process, I have seen a dramatic change in their desires. Their home teaching efforts rise from negligent to 100 percent. Prayer and scripture study return to the home and meaningful Family Home Evenings resume. The priesthood holders bear testimonies that have been

silent for many years. Men who previously approached church casu-
ally become committed, front-half-of-the-chapel, arrive-ten-minutes-
early, white-shirt-and-tie members. They desire to serve. They desire
to teach. They desire to magnify their callings. They desire to seek
righteousness. They desire to share the gospel. They desire to keep all
of the commandments of the Lord. They can be counted on.

These righteous desires are evident wherever true repentance
has occurred; repentance leaves people humble and teachable. In the
Sermon on the Mount, Jesus taught the principle, "Blessed are they
which do hunger and thirst after righteousness; for they shall be filled"
(Matthew 5:6).

To "hunger and thirst" encompasses our most basic desires. The
scriptures detail many instances where people have hungered and
thirst after righteous desires:

> And, finding there was greater happiness and peace and rest
> for me, *I sought for the blessings of the fathers*, and the right whereunto
> I should be ordained to administer the same; having been myself a
> follower of righteousness, *desiring also to be one who possessed great
> knowledge, and to be a greater follower of righteousness, and to possess
> a greater knowledge*, and to be a father of many nations, a prince of
> peace, *and desiring to receive instructions, and to keep the commandments
> of God*, I became a rightful heir, a High Priest, holding the right
> belonging to the fathers. (Abraham 1:2, emphasis added)

> And again Moses said: I will not cease to call upon God, *I have
> other things to inquire of him.* (Moses 1:18, emphasis added)

> And *my soul hungered*; and I kneeled down before my Maker,
> and I cried unto him in mighty prayer and supplication for mine
> own soul; and all the day long did I cry unto him; yea, and when the
> night came I did still raise my voice high that it reached the heavens.
> (Enos 1:4, emphasis added)

> *O that I were an angel, and could have the wish of my heart, that I
> might go forth and speak with the trump of God*, with a voice to shake
> the earth, and cry repentance unto every people!
> Yea, I would declare unto every soul, as with the voice of thun-
> der, repentance and the plan of redemption, that they should repent
> and come unto our God, that there might not be more sorrow upon
> all the face of the earth. (Alma 29:1–2, emphasis added)

After I had retired to the place where I had previously designed to go, having looked around me and finding myself alone, *I kneeled down and began to offer up the desires of my heart to God.* (JS–H 1:15, emphasis added)

These desires are not inconsequential, and they are not reserved only for prophets. They come from men and women who have known and experienced the power of repentance in their own lives. We too can gain these desires when we repent.

CONFORMING TO PROMPTINGS

As Heavenly Father's children pray to Him for assistance—for help in times of need, for guidance, for direction, for intervention on their behalf or on behalf of a loved one, or for needed blessings—He frequently answers those prayers through the actions of others. He sends His servants directly to those in need, even though we often don't understand what others can do for us.

Sometimes the ministering of angels comes from the other side of the veil, but God frequently sends his mortal angels to us. Nephi taught that "angels speak by the power of the Holy Ghost; wherefore they speak the words of Christ" (2 Nephi 32:3). When someone speaks by the power of the Holy Ghost, saying what Christ would say, they speak with the tongue of angels (2 Nephi 32:2). Angels are God's messengers. They are people on either side of the veil whom the Lord entrusts to deliver his words and carry out his will.

To gain this special responsibility, we must prepare ourselves to learn the words our Heavenly Father would have us say. "For behold, again I say unto you that if you will enter in by the way, and receive the Holy Ghost, it will be shown you all things what ye should do" (2 Nephi 32:5).

The Holy Ghost blesses those who have humbled themselves through repentance and who desire to work righteousness. The Lord trusts these diligent people and bestows to them the promptings of the still, small voice to aid in responding to the needs of others. When we respond immediately to these promptings, we demonstrate to the Lord that we are worthy of His trust. We become as instruments in the Lord's hands to help answer someone's prayer.

Elder Henry B. Eyring, an Apostle of the Lord, addresses this principle within the context of repentance:

You might, in addition, be eager to conform to the quiet prompt-ings that urge you to take action. Make a commitment that the next time you are taught by one of the servants of God, you will heed any prompting, even the faintest prompting, to act, to do better. In fact, you could commit to opening your heart to those promptings even while reading these words. *That also is the spirit of repentance.*

I had that happen to me not long ago. I was sitting in my home ward in the presence of a teacher who said something, and I felt a very faint prompting from the Spirit to act that day. I bear you my testimony that the scriptures are not being poetic when they describe the Holy Ghost as the still, small voice. It is so quiet that if you are noisy inside, you won't hear it. It is real. I felt also that if I didn't do it promptly, I would not again, at least not soon, feel that gentle instruction. So I did it. I am confident that because I went and did the small thing that I felt impressed by the quiet voice to do, I made it more likely that I could receive a spiritual nudge again

I pray that you will make a commitment to act on those prompt-ings you receive when listening to your teachers and leaders. If you feel a prompting to do something as a result of reading this book [*To Draw Closer to God*], and if you do it, you will reinforce in your life a pattern of repentance—which is to be eager to be instructed, even to be reproved, and then to act.[2]

Like Elder Eyring, I have also felt the promptings of the still, small voice in my life. I have found that when I immediately respond to those promptings, I am more likely to receive them again. The Lord sends those whom He trusts to be His hands, His feet, and His voice in answering the prayers of His children.

I will never forget the feeling I had one Thursday night as I sat in a stake training meeting. Surely the stake president and his counselors gave wonderful, spiritual presentations, full of necessary instruction. But I don't remember a word of it because I was distracted.

I was a relatively new bishop, and I had not yet met every member of my ward. I knew all of the active members and many of the less active ones. Still, several members were only names to me. That night, I couldn't get one of the names out of my mind. All I knew was that he and his wife were retired and never came to church.

The Spirit said to me, "Go and see him."

---

2.   Henry B. Eyring, *To Draw Closer to God: A Collection of Discourses*, (Salt Lake City: Deseret Book) 18; emphasis added.

I responded, "Not right now; I'm in a meeting."

I thought, *I am where I am supposed to be now. I am listening to the stake president give me important instruction in a priesthood meeting. What could be more important? It would be rude of me to leave.*

Semi-confident that I had made an important point, I continued to sit through the rest of the meeting. I told myself that if I was really supposed to visit this member, the meeting would finish early enough to give me time to stop by afterward. The Spirit did not relent, but neither did I.

I sat and watched the clock on the wall as the hour grew later and later. Just before eleven o'clock, the meeting concluded. I told myself that it was too late to stop by that night but that I would try to call in the morning.

My direct route home would take me immediately past this member's house. As I approached the member's home, the Spirit told me again to stop and see him. I slowed down a little as I looked at the house and found no sign of activity. "They are already asleep," I said to myself as I drove home.

I pulled in to my driveway and took the key out of the ignition. Now, the Spirit was screaming at me—in a still, small voice sort of way. I put the key back in the ignition, backed out of the driveway, and drove back to the member's home. As I pulled up in front of the house, I thought, *What am I going to say to them? They don't even know me!*

I cleared my tight throat and rang the doorbell. The man answered and invited me in. He and his wife were not asleep; they were in the back part of the house discussing important things. And it turned out that they needed me that night.

I am certain that, given my wrestling match with the Spirit, if the Lord had anyone else to send, He would have. But this couple needed their bishop, and no one else would have sufficed. I learned a very important lesson that night, and I vowed that I would never again fight the promptings of the Spirit. I had some repenting to do.

By knocking on that door, even though I didn't know why at the time, I accomplished the Lord's work. Likewise, when we don't act immediately on the promptings we receive, the opportunity may pass. Those lost opportunities generally do not return to us again. Hearts that were once softened for a moment become hardened again. People move away, change, and even die before we get the chance to touch their lives. It is our sacred responsibility to follow the promptings of the Spirit "in the season thereof."

FORGIVING OTHERS

One of the most basic elements of Christ's doctrine, taught repeatedly in the Bible, the Book of Mormon, and modern revelation, requires as parties to the everlasting covenant—or the covenant of the Atonement—to forgive others. The scriptures teach us that as we forgive, we will be forgiven; likewise, as we judge others, so will we be judged. Here is but a sampling of the scriptures' admonition to forgive:

And forgive us our debts, as we forgive our debtors. . . .
For if ye forgive men their trespasses, your heavenly Father will also forgive you:
But if ye forgive not men their trespasses, neither will your Father forgive your trespasses. (Matthew 6:12, 14–15)

Judge not unrighteously, that ye be not judged.
For with what judgment ye judge, ye shall be judged: but judge righteous judgment and with what measure ye mete, it shall be measured to you again. (JST Matthew 7:1–2)

Then came Peter to him, and said, Lord, how oft shall my brother sin against me, and I forgive him? Till seven times?
Jesus saith unto him, I say not unto thee, Until seven times: but, Until seventy times seven. (Matthew 18:21–22)

And ye shall also forgive one another your trespasses; for verily I say unto you, he that forgiveth not his neighbor's trespasses when he says that he repents, the same hath brought himself under condemnation. (Mosiah 26:31)

So likewise shall my heavenly Father do also unto you, if ye from your hearts forgive not every one his brother their trespasses. (Matthew 18:35)

And now, my brethren, seeing that ye know the light by which ye may judge, which light is the light of Christ, see that ye do not judge wrongfully; for with that same judgment which ye judge ye shall also be judged. (Moroni 7:18)

And when ye stand praying, forgive, if ye have ought against any: that your Father also which is in heaven may forgive you your trespasses.
But if ye do not forgive, neither will your Father which is in heaven forgive your trespasses. (Mark 11:25–26)

And forgive us our sins; for we also forgive every one that is
indebted to us. And lead us not into temptation; but deliver us from
evil. (Luke 11:14)

And again, verily I say unto you, if after thine enemy has come
upon thee praying thy forgiveness, thou shalt forgive him and shalt
hold it no more as a testimony against thine enemy—and so on unto
the second and third time—
And as oft as thine enemy repenteth of the trespass wherewith
he has trespassed against thee, thou shalt forgive him, until seventy
times seven. (D&C 98:39–40)

For, if ye forgive men their trespasses your heavenly Father will
also forgive you;
But if ye forgive not men their trespasses neither will your
Father forgive your trespasses. (3 Nephi 13:14–15)

Wherefore, I say unto you, that ye ought to forgive one another;
for he that forgiveth not his brother his trespasses standeth condemned before the Lord; for there remaineth in him the greater sin.
(D&C 64:9)

Forgiving others is a prerequisite to obtaining forgiveness ourselves, but it is also one of the fruits of repentance. If the process of
repentance results in the type of transcendent change of heart that
Alma describes, and if true repentance results in a new, personal com-
prehension of the reality of the Atonement, then it naturally follows
that one who has received the blessed gift of forgiveness would mirror
that same forgiveness in their dealings with others.

When we readily forgive others, we become a living witness of the
reality of the Savior's sacrifice and forgiveness. Conversely, when we
harbor bitterness, anger, and resentment toward others, we reject the
Saviors sacrifices; we become as those described by Nephi:

For the things which some men esteem to be of great worth, both
to the body and soul, others set at naught and trample under their
feet. Yea, even the very God of Israel do men trample under their feet;
I say, trample under their feet but I would speak in other words—they
set him at naught and hearken not to the voice of his counsels. . . .
And the world, because of their iniquity, shall judge him to be
a thing of naught; wherefore they scourge him, and he suffereth it;
and they smite him, and he suffereth it. Yea, they spit upon him, and
he suffereth it, because of his loving kindness and his long-suffering

towards the children of men. (1 Nephi 19:7, 9)

By refusing to forgive others, we ignore the Lord's counsel and trample Him under our feet. When we carry grudges, we act as though other people have wronged us in a way that makes them unworthy of our forgiveness. Sometimes we even believe in our hearts that the Lord's forgiveness cannot touch those who have inexcusably hurt us. We then invoke the eternal law: the standard we apply to others is applied to us. In that emotional and spiritual state, we may not understand that the Atonement is actually null and void to us.

When we truly seek forgiveness from the absolute depths of humility, we feel as though in that moment that there is no other soul on earth more unworthy of the Lord's mercy than we are. When we finally receive that forgiveness, we feel the burden lifted and we rejoice. How could we deny another person our forgiveness and mercy when we so desperately yearn for the Lord's? When we deny others this special gift, we become as an unmerciful servant:

> Therefore is the kingdom of heaven likened unto a certain king, which would take account of his servants.
>
> And when he had begun to reckon, one was brought unto him, which owed him ten thousand talents.
>
> But forasmuch as he had not to pay, his lord commanded him to be sold, and his wife, and children, and all that he had, and payment to be made.
>
> The servant therefore fell down, and worshipped him, saying, Lord, have patience with me, and I will pay thee all.
>
> Then the lord of that servant was moved with compassion, and loosed him, and forgave him the debt.
>
> But the same servant went out, and found one of his fellowservants, which owed him an hundred pence: and he laid hands on him, and took him by the throat, saying, Pay me that thou owest.
>
> And his fellowservant fell down at his feet, and besought him, saying, Have patience with me, and I will pay thee all.
>
> And he would not: but went and cast him into prison, till he should pay the debt. . . .
>
> Then his lord, after that he had called him said unto him, O thou wicked servant, I forgave thee all that debt, because thou desirest me:
>
> Shouldest not thou also have had compassion on thy fellowservant, even as I had pity on thee? (Matthew 18:23–30, 32–33)

The answer to the Lord's rhetorical question is, "Of course!" When we have been forgiven, we should have compassion on our fellow men. It is a covenant obligation of His Saints.

The prophet Alma suggests that when we are "spiritually born of God," receive "his image in [our] countenances," experience "this mighty change in [our] hearts," and exercise "faith in the redemption," we will "sing the song of redeeming love" (Alma 5:14–15, 26). With that song fresh in our changed hearts, how can we then turn and "make a mock of [our] brother" or "heap upon him persecutions"? (Alma 5:30). Yet that is precisely what we do by our refusal to forgive others and put our anger, our bitterness, and our internal darkness behind us.

True repentance sanctifies and purifies. A pure heart exudes pure love. "Charity, the pure love of Christ, suffereth long" (1 Corinthians 13:4). A pure soul forgives. In fact, the very meaning of the word "forgive" is to "give first" or "give in advance," which is consistent with the words of John Taylor, a prophet of God, when he taught that "forgiveness is in advance of justice."

In other words, forgiveness comes first. We must forgive others even before they recognize their sins, acknowledge their mistakes, or make restitution. Indeed, the principle of forgiveness as taught by the Savior is actually a state of being—not of what we do, but of who we are: "Blessed are the merciful: for they shall obtain mercy" (Matthew 5:7).

TESTIMONY AND WITNESS OF THE ATONEMENT

"Retain a remission of your sins; and ye shall grow in the knowledge of the glory of him that created you, or in the knowledge of that which is just and true" (Mosiah 4:12). Repentance is a personal process. As I have counseled others concerning repentance, I have explained that the labor of repentance rests on the shoulders of the person who seeks it rather than the Lord. I have said something like this:

"My role as your bishop is to ensure that you have done everything that you are capable of and everything that is necessary to receive forgiveness from your Savior. I will give you assignments and counsel, and you will return and report your progress to me. As you obey this counsel and fulfill your assignments, the time will eventually come when you and I will set this matter behind us, and we will never speak of it again. If formal disciplinary action is necessary to assist you through full repentance—if you are humble and obedient—the time will come when that too will be concluded. However, please understand that as your bishop I do not and cannot grant forgiveness; those keys were never given to man. I cannot tell you when the Lord has accepted your offering. However, you have a right to know by personal revelation that you have been forgiven. That time may come before or after you and I complete this process together; but if you are truly repentant, humble, and obedient, the time will come when you shall know that the Lord has accepted your sacrifice and that He has forgiven you."

This knowledge and testimony is the great reward of the gospel of Jesus Christ. But it only comes to those who have paid the price.

It is possible, I believe, for someone to make a change in their life without following the repentance process. It is also possible—probably far too often—that those who have entered into the everlasting covenant treat the repentance process far too lightly. In fact, for some Saints, the longer they belong to the Church, the more likely they are to participate in its processes because of tradition or other people's expectations rather than because of the doctrine of repentance. Most of us have been guilty of outward observance while failing to attend to essential inward repentance, but it is our responsibility to ensure that our repentance is genuine.

Our society is accustomed to receiving immediate solutions to problems, and the Saints are not immune to this temptation. Nevertheless, repentance is the antithesis of instant gratification. There is no shortcut to true repentance—although we may wish there were—just as there was no shortcut to the atoning sacrifice. Even Christ asked if the cup might pass from Him: "And he said, Abba, Father, all things are possible unto thee; take away this cup from me: nevertheless not what I will, but what thou wilt" (Mark 14:36).

The presence of the Aramaic word *Abba* in the Greek-based text of the New Testament is significant. In Aramaic, *Abba* means "father," but Hebrew speakers use the word as a personal, familiar term for one's father.[3] This is similar to the way we use "daddy" in English. This sheds light on the depth of Christ's pleadings with the Father that the cup be removed. His submissive declaration that "nevertheless not what I will, but what thou wilt" is so much more telling in that intensely personal context. Jesus was willing to submit to the will of the Father in all things so that the Atonement could benefit all humanity. We must try to submit our will to the Father when we repent of our

---

3. Bible Dictionary, "Abba," 600.

sins, just as Christ did when he suffered and atoned for them.

Guilt and godly sorrow are not the same thing. Too often we are motivated in our repentance by guilt and seldom attain godly sorrow. As a result, it is common for us to think we have repented simply because we have changed a few things about ourselves. Changing our habits can help us overcome guilt without experiencing the godly sorrow that brings us closer to Christ. When we lack this powerful gift, it is difficult to know whether we have received a personal testimony of the Savior and his atoning sacrifice.

The personal witness of the Savior and of receiving forgiveness is the ultimate fruit of repentance. It is a fundamental reason why we are granted a probationary period to repent in the first place: in so doing, we gain our own unique testimony of the reality of the Atonement. The testimony of the Savior is a reward of repentance, received by revelation, which becomes the rock to which we anchor our souls. The scriptures indicate that if we have been taught the gospel but never receive this personal testimony of the Savior while we're on earth, the blessings of the celestial kingdom elude us, and the best we can hope for is a terrestrial resurrection (D&C 76:74).

Armed with this specific, intimate knowledge and assurance that belongs only to you—that can be received only from God—no one can shake your faith in the Savior. After Alma's experiences, nobody could talk him out of his knowledge of Christ. So can it be with us.

When we have personally experienced our burden lifted, our guilt removed, our stains erased, and our garments "washed white through the blood of the Lamb" (Alma 13:11), and when feelings of anguish and suffering that only we and the Savior can fully understand are taken from us and replaced with comfort, peace, and joy, then we cannot be dissuaded from our knowledge that Jesus Christ lives. We come to know that He is the Christ, the Only Begotten Son of the Father. We gain a knowledge that He has forgiven us, that He willingly suffered, bled, and died for our sins, and that the keys of the gospel of repentance have been restored to the earth and through its ordinances we have access to the covenant of the Atonement in these latter days.

"If any man will do his will, he shall know of the doctrine, whether it be of God, or whether I speak of myself" (John 7:17).

CHAPTER TWO
Second Only to Faith

I know that which the Lord hath commanded me, and I glory in it. I do not glory of myself, but I glory in that which the Lord hath commanded me; yea, and this is my glory, that perhaps I may be an instrument in the hands of God to bring some soul to repentance; and this is my joy.

—Alma 29:9

REPENTANCE IS OFTEN THOUGHT OF AS A HARD doctrine, enforced only by the heavy hand of discipline. We often feel that the doctrine of repentance seems condemnatory and chastising instead of uplifting and edifying. Perhaps we feel this way because the natural man does not give much serious attention to the doctrine of repentance until chastisement is already upon him. But the call to repentance is the call of the Shepherd. It is the call of loving protection from the dangers of the world by the One who has laid down His life for His lost sheep.

A young woman in my ward came to see me one Sunday afternoon. She was troubled by the typical problems of a person her age. While she had not been involved in any serious sin, she felt rebellion and frustration with what she viewed as a Church that focused on all the things she should not do. She wanted to do what was right, but she was having difficulty understanding why the Church made such a "big deal" out of so many "little things."

From her perspective, the Church had taken all of the freedom of expression out of life. That is a common complaint for members who struggle with worldly challenges. However, what exactly constitutes "little things" varies considerably, depending upon the individual. Thing are not always as "little" as they seem. For this young woman, her "little things" included such issues as dressing modestly, "having to" have friends who share her values, and having only one set of earrings.

We had a long talk. We agreed that there are many instances in which we, as members of the Church, wrongly judge others based on whether their hair is too long, their dress is too short, or they have a tattoo. We agreed that there are many good people in the world who don't meet our visual standards for righteousness, while many Church members "talk the talk but don't walk the walk."

I shared with her the words of Paul as he addressed the issue of Church members eating the meat that had been offered to idols. Paul made the same point as this young woman when he said, "Meat commendeth us not to God: for neither if we eat, are we the better, neither if we eat not, are we the worse" (1 Corinthians 8:8). He could easily have said that earrings commendeth us not to God or hairstyles commendeth us not to God. The fashion of the world commendeth us not to God. What we wear doesn't make us intrinsically good or bad. We can use that argument to justify a lot of things that are not in harmony with the teachings of the Church.

However, as we followed Paul's teachings and spoke of what happens within us and to others when our hearts turn to Christ and the gospel, we learned some important principles. We talked about the example we set when our inward desire for righteousness doesn't match our outward, visual standards; this can damage those who watch us who are weak in faith. Paul continues:

> But take heed lest by any means this liberty of yours become a stumblingblock to them that are weak.
>
> For if any man see thee which hast knowledge sit at meat in the idol's temple, shall not the conscience of him which is weak be emboldened to eat those things which are offered to idols;
>
> And through thy knowledge shall the weak brother perish, for whom Christ died?
>
> But when ye sin so against the brethren, and wound their weak conscience, ye sin against Christ. (1 Corinthians 8:9–12)

We then discussed our agency and the inherent responsibility that we bear in exercising it—responsibility not only to our Heavenly Father but also to our friends and neighbors. We spoke of avoiding the appearance of evil by staying away from the things about which the prophets of God have warned us. Then we talked about the principle of repentance and how coming to Christ changes our hearts. When we have a heart single to Christ and the gospel, the "little things" that once troubled us no longer really matter.

Before we finished our conversation, this wonderful young woman saw more clearly that there is a lot more to living the gospel than obeying harsh rules and austere commandments, and that we don't repent just because God will punish us if we don't. It is true that the commandments are strict, and God has warned us about what will happen if we don't repent. But the transition from a proud heart to an obedient heart is such a marvelous thing! This is where we find the true beauty in the gospel.

Of all the basic principles of the gospel of Jesus Christ, repentance is probably the most difficult to realize. It requires more love, patience, and hope, and requires more of the "tender mercies of the Lord" (1 Nephi 1:20) than perhaps any other. Repentance unlocks the blessings of heaven more than anything else we are commanded to do. Although chastisement from the Lord will certainly come when necessary, we must perpetually seek a better understanding of the doctrine of repentance and how it affects both our short-term happiness and our long-term joy. We must learn of the blessings of repentance as we walk in obedience so the shadow of our immediate sin cannot not cloud our perspective. The more we learn about the blessings and processes of repentance when we are without sin, the more effective our repentance can be when we need to exercise it—and we all unavoidably need to exercise it.

When we understand repentance in righteousness, we become better people; we are more obedient, more faith-filled, more loving, more caring, more humble, and more content. As we make repentance a consistent, present priority in our lives, we live within a perspective that allows us to see the arm of the Lord continually stretched out in our behalf. When we have this perspective, our faith is increased and our vision will include the things of God.

A perpetual understanding of repentance leads to a cycle of righteousness. We develop faith in God, which leads us to a desire to repent of our sins when we need to. Our repentance is eventually rewarded with assurances of the Spirit, and our faith is increased. With increased faith and vision, we are able to see what we need to change about ourselves, and we can repent and come further unto Christ. And that repentance is further rewarded with even greater faith. This challenging but rewarding cycle, repeated throughout life, fulfills the divine intent of perfection: first faith, and second repentance.

THE FIRST PRINCIPLES AND ORDINANCES OF THE GOSPEL

When the Prophet Joseph Smith outlined the precepts of the newly restored Church of Jesus Christ to a curious John Wentworth, editor and owner of the *Chicago Democrat,* he did not address the mysteries of heaven or explore the depths or breadths of restored doctrine. He was neither defensive in his approach nor critical of the beliefs of others. He dealt only with the basics.

The Articles of Faith, penned in that early setting, provided then to Wentworth—and now to the world—a brief outline of our most basic beliefs, divided into thirteen separate statements. In the fourth article of faith, Joseph Smith focused not on all gospel doctrine but on only the *first* principles and ordinances of the gospel, which Primary children recite around the world: "We believe that the first principles and ordinances of the gospel are: first, Faith in the Lord Jesus Christ; second, Repentance; third, Baptism by immersion for the remission of sins; fourth, Laying on of hands for the gift of the Holy Ghost."

Without any additional comment or explanation, the Prophet declared that repentance is the second principle of the gospel of Jesus Christ. The specified order outlined in the fourth article of faith suggests what the scriptures repeatedly teach: understanding, believing, and acting upon the name of the Lord Jesus Christ brings the natural man to a painful awareness of his sin-filled state. True faith—a principle of action, as Joseph Smith taught—leads one directly to repentance. "And if ye will believe on his name ye will repent of all your sins, that thereby ye may have a remission of them through his merits" (Helaman 14:13).

But what is repentance? Easton's Bible Dictionary suggests these definitions from the Greek words used in the New Testament:

1. *Metamelomai* is a verb used to refer to a change of mind which results in regret or even remorse on account of sin, but not necessarily a change of heart. Interestingly, this is the word used with reference to the repentance of Judas Iscariot.

2. *Metanoeo* means to change one's mind and purpose as the result of knowledge. This verb, with the cognate noun *metanoia*, is used to describe true repentance: a change of mind, purpose, and life, to which remission of sin is promised.

In the context of the principles and ordinances of the gospel, repentance changes not only our mind (*metamelomai*), understanding, and purpose (*metanoeo*) but also our heart and our desires. These terms contain the prefix *meta*, which in these words denotes a condition after a change. This is the same prefix used in the word *metamorphosis*, which means "a complete change in physical form or substance." True, sincere repentance changes our very essence. It redefines *who* we are and *why* we exist. It changes our purposes, our intentions, and our desires. We are changed in appearance and essence.

> Because all accountable men are stained by sin and because no unclean thing can enter into the kingdom of heaven, a merciful God has ordained the *law of repentance* whereby the human soul may be cleansed and conditioned for eternal life in his everlasting presence. Repentance is the process whereby a mortal soul—unclean and stained with the guilt of sin—is enabled to cast off the burden of guilt, wash away the filth of iniquity, and become clean every whit, entirely free from the bondage of sin.[1]

THE EXPERIENCE OF ALMA THE YOUNGER

Alma the Younger knew intimately the price and value of repentance, so he preached eloquently to the people of the Church in the land of Zarahemla. Alma was well acquainted with repentance and the change that results from it. His words carried weight with the people because he taught through the power of his personal knowledge and experience. In fact, his words still carry this significant power many centuries later as the Spirit testifies to us of the truthfulness of his words.

The people of Zarahemla knew all about the errors of Alma's earlier ways. In later years, as he recounted the experiences of his youth to his son, Helaman, he told how he had spent much of his rebellious years going about "seeking to destroy the Church of God" (Alma 36:6). Alma

---

1. Bruce R. McConkie, *Mormon Doctrine*, 2nd ed., (Salt Lake City: Bookcraft, 1966) 630.

and the other sons of Mosiah were involved in far more serious and damaging behavior than mere teenage pranks. It is likely that these men were old enough, mature enough, and well-respected enough that their words and their works greatly influenced the community. They, like Satan, were rebelling against the work of the fathers. However, like Saul of Tarsus, the Lord had another work for them to do and brought an immediate and dramatic interruption to the damage they were causing: "but behold, God sent his holy angel to stop [him] by the way" (Alma 36:6).

When the angel spoke "as it were with the voice of thunder," the "whole earth did tremble," and the scripture records that Alma and his companions "fell to the earth for the fear of the Lord" (Alma 36:7). The angel told Alma that though he was free to use his agency to destroy himself, he would not be allowed to destroy the Church of God and exercise such a devastating influence over its members.

Upon hearing the angel's words, Alma collapsed to the ground, was carried to his father, and lay for three days and three nights—most likely unaware that his unconsciousness represented Christ's death and Resurrection. He was paralyzed with "fear and amazement" concerning the significance and consequence of his actions (Alma 36:11). He was stunned to learn that all of his father's supposed foolishness about religion was actually rooted in a real, powerful gospel. The consequences of Alma's actions were suddenly right before him.

Alma recounted this powerful experience in a memorable and touching testimony written for his son Helaman, who may have experienced similar challenges of his own. Alma described—as best he could with the limitations of language and the nuances of his thoughts—the feelings and pain he endured as he lay on the ground:

> I was racked with eternal torment, for my soul was harrowed up to the greatest degree and racked with all my sins.
>
> Yea, I did remember all my sins and iniquities, for which I was tormented with the pains of hell; yea, I saw that I had rebelled against God, and that I had not kept his holy commandments.
>
> Yea, I had . . . led [His children] away unto destruction; yea, and in fine so great had been my iniquities, that the very thought of coming into the presence of my God did rack my soul with inexpressible horror.
>
> Oh, thought I, that I could be banished and become extinct both

soul and body, that I might not be brought to stand in the presence of my God, to be judged of my deeds.

And now, for three days and for three nights was I racked with the pains of a damned soul.

And it came to pass that as I was thus racked with torment, while I was harrowed up by the memory of my many sins, behold, I remembered also to have heard my father prophesy unto the people concerning the coming of one Jesus Christ, a Son of God, to atone for the sins of the world.

Now, as my mind caught hold upon this thought, I cried within my heart: O Jesus, thou Son of God, have mercy on me, who am in the gall of bitterness, and am encircled about by the everlasting chains of death.

And now, behold, when I thought this, I could remember my pains no more; yea, I was harrowed up by the memory of my sins no more.

And oh, what joy, and what marvelous light I did behold; yea, my soul was filled with joy as exceeding as was my pain! (Alma 36:12–20)

Certainly, Alma knew something about repentance. He was, in fact, an expert on the subject. So, when he taught the people of the Church in the land of Zarahemla, he did so with the knowledge and authority gained from firsthand experience, not simply from theory. He knew intensely and intimately about godly sorrow, remorse, and contrition. He knew about the need for restitution for the damage he had done, and he dedicated the rest of his life to it. He also knew about what repentance does to and for the penitent:

And now behold, I ask of you, my brethren of the Church, have ye spiritually been born of God? Have ye received his image in your countenances? Have ye experienced this mighty change in your hearts? (Alma 5:14)

And now behold, I say unto you, my brethren, if ye have experienced a change of heart, and if ye have felt to sing the song of redeeming love, I would ask, can ye feel so now? (Alma 5:26)

I say unto you, that I know that Jesus Christ shall come, yea, the Son, the Only Begotten of the Father, full of grace and truth. And behold, it is he that cometh to take away the sins of the world, yea the sins of every man who steadfastly believeth on his name. (Alma 5:48)

To Alma, repentance was not merely the changing of one's mind. Nor was it simply changing his actions. It was a complete rebirth with a new heart, with the image of God visible in his countenance. And it required then, as it does today, more than just a singular or even occasional event in the life of the sinner. It requires man to constantly answer the question affirmatively, "Can ye feel so now?"

Alma's testimony of the Atonement of Jesus Christ was certain. Though it had not yet come to pass, Alma knew of its reality, seeing it with an eye of faith. For us, the Atonement is an event of the past, but we must have the same type of faith that Alma had. We must see it with the very same eye of faith that Alma had. The great sacrifice has already been made. Through repentance, we can know for ourselves, just as Alma did, that He came "to take away the sins of the world, yea the sins of every man who steadfastly believeth on his name."

True repentance requires great effort, sacrifice, and sometimes pain. From Alma's words, it is clear that he experienced personal suffering as he underwent his remarkable transformation through the repentance process. However, his suffering pales in comparison to that which would have been required of him had he not repented.

> Every man must repent or suffer. In the event of repentance, the law of mercy prevails, and the penitent are saved from suffering. "I, God, have suffered these things for all, that they might not suffer if they would repent; But if they would not repent they must suffer even as I; Which suffering caused myself, even God, the greatest of all, to tremble because of pain, and to bleed at every pore, and to suffer both body and spirit" (D&C 19:4–20). Hence comes the Lord's imperative command to repent. Where there is no repentance, the law of justice takes precedence and remission of sins is gained through suffering rather than as a gift of God through the blood of Christ.[2]

"And the rebellious shall be pierced with much sorrow" (D&C 1:3). And yet, the scriptures do not say that "men are that they might have sorrow." Sorrow is not the purpose of our existence. It is not God's intention that we stagnate in a pool of sadness and suffering, for it does nothing to move us toward immortality and eternal life. We are not fulfilled in sorrow and suffering. We are fulfilled in joy because the Savior has provided a way and has redeemed us:

---

2. McConkie, *Mormon Doctrine*, 631.

Adam fell that men might be; and men are, that they might have joy.

And the Messiah cometh in the fulness of time, that he may redeem the children of men from the fall. And because that they are redeemed from the fall they have become free forever, knowing good from evil; to act for themselves and not to be acted upon, save it be by the punishment of the law at the great and last day, according to the commandments which God hath given. (2 Nephi 2:25–26)

SAY NOTHING BUT REPENTANCE

As the message of the Restoration goes to the world, the Lord's messengers are commanded to "say nothing but repentance unto this generation" (D&C 6:9). It is not God's desire that we should suffer, as evidenced by the very presence of the merciful plan of salvation that provides a Redeemer and Savior for us. Jesus taught that those who are prepared will receive this message and recognize its divine source as from the true Shepherd. "My sheep hear my voice, and I know them, and they follow me" (John 10:27).

As His sheep, disciples of Christ are blessed with the capacity to recognize the voice of Deity. And more than that, His sheep have a deep, abiding desire to follow their Shepherd. We do that by accepting His teachings, living His commandments, and making and keeping sacred covenants—starting with baptism.

So, by receiving the gospel into our lives, whether as a new convert or as one born into the Church, we are actually accepting and applying the principle of repentance in our lives. But to do so, we cannot merely change our minds. We do not simply decide that we will now attend this church rather than that one. We do not simply choose to change our previous destructive, unhealthy habits and replace them with new and better ones. Anyone can make those kinds of choices, even without the power of the atoning sacrifice. Instead, we must change our being. We must be reborn, as Alma was, with God's image in our countenances. We must change our hearts, minds, intentions, and desires. This is the process by which we come unto Christ and become like Him. After all, that is the great and majestic purpose of the Atonement: to become "at one" with our Heavenly Father and our Savior.

By truly repenting, we prepare to take upon ourselves sacred covenants and receive promised blessings. In the fourth article of faith, repentance is followed by the sacred covenant of baptism and the sanctifying blessing of the gift of the Holy Ghost. This is the pattern by which our Heavenly Father works with His children. The covenant-blessing relationship is one that will sanctify our lives daily here on earth and exalt us throughout the eternities.

There are many sacred covenants beyond baptism. The scriptures set forth a multitude of promised blessings for His covenant people. One common key unlocks the door to all of these sacred blessings, covenants, and godly gifts; that key is repentance.

CHAPTER THREE
The Keys of Repentance

And the lesser priesthood continued, which priesthood holdeth the key of the ministering of angels and the preparatory gospel; Which gospel is the gospel of repentance and of baptism, and the remission of sins.

—Doctrine and Covenants 84:26–27

I WAS RECENTLY REMINDED OF THE DEGREE IN which my life relies on holding the proper keys. I'm afraid I generally take this for granted in both my spiritual and temporal life. All I needed to freshen my appreciation for these keys was to lose them. Perhaps you have had an experience similar to mine.

Recently my wife and I scheduled a "play day" in the desert for our family. My teenage sons cleared their busy weekend schedules, and early Saturday morning we loaded our coolers with sandwiches, sodas, and an assortment of snacks—which we affectionately call "Poagie Bait," a term that I learned from my father. We had a wonderful time riding motorcycles and four-wheelers over miles of winding trails that extended between two states.

As the day drew to a close, we gathered all of our gear and loaded the machines on our trailer. We were a good kind of dirty and had completely enjoyed the time we had spent together. Our conversation was happy and light. I reached into my pocket for my truck keys so we could drive home and have dinner.

No keys. Somewhere in the wilderness of southern Utah—or possibly northern Arizona—my keys had slipped from my pocket and undoubtedly lay partially buried in some obscure section of desert. Talk about a needle in a haystack! We searched for them briefly, but acknowledging the limited odds of finding them, we soon abandoned our efforts. I might as well have dropped them into Lake Powell (which is another story).

Fortunately, my wife, Genine, provided a backup set of keys to our truck, which prevented us from spending an unplanned night in the desert. But only as I considered each of the individual keys that were on my lost key chain did I realize—and appreciate—what I had actually lost.

Each lost key was symbolic of a specific and important aspect of my life. I lost keys to all of my vehicles, which represent my mobility, my access to the world, and my freedom of movement. I lost the keys to my home—our haven from the world's influences—which provides my family with shelter and protection. I lost keys to my office, which allow me to earn a living to support my family's temporal needs. I lost my key chain pass card to a local gym, which represents my health and physical well-being. I also lost a variety of smaller keys to miscellaneous locks that I don't remember until I actually need them again.

Those lost keys embody so many of the important things that I take for granted. I noted in frustration that while I still had my automobiles, home, and office, I couldn't actually use any of them until I made new keys. My access to essential aspects of my life was gone. Replacing those keys has been neither easy nor inexpensive.

Priesthood keys give us similar access to specific blessings and to precise and essential aspects of Christ's atoning power. The Atonement of Jesus Christ, and the blessings that come from it, exist as eternal realities. However, our right to access some of these particular powers and blessings depends upon the presence of specifically connected priesthood keys turned on our behalf—and at the appropriate time—by authorized administrators of the gospel of Jesus Christ. This is part of the "line upon line, precept upon precept" principle, which allows us to prepare ourselves to take each step back to our Heavenly Father's presence through Christ's sacrifice.

We simply aren't ready to receive everything at once. Therefore, in His wisdom, God has placed child-proof locks on each of the blessings that are accompanied by additional responsibility and accountability. In this way, we are protected from being held prematurely accountable for things we are not prepared to receive. Priesthood keys are required to open these locks.

Moreover, those who wish to open the locks for others must hold not only hold the priesthood, but also the specific keys necessary for each unique lock. These keys are bestowed following the pattern of scripture: by the laying on of hands by one who has the authority. Primary among those specified priesthood keys are the keys to administer the gospel of repentance and its associated ordinances on the earth.

BEGINNING THE RESTORATION

In May of 1829, John the Baptist appeared to Joseph Smith and Oliver Cowdery on the banks of the Susquehanna River near Harmony, Pennsylvania. Joseph and Oliver had been translating the Book of Mormon when they came upon passages that referred to baptism. They were inspired to inquire of the Lord regarding what authority is necessary to perform these ordinances, so they fervently sought an answer.

Nearly two millennia earlier, the angel Gabriel had announced to Zacharias, father of John the Baptist, the forthcoming birth and mission of his son. Prophets had spoken reverently of his role in preparing the way for the mission of Jesus Christ. When John was only eight days old, an angel ordained him to prepare the people for the coming of the Lord.

John the Baptist was born into a priestly lineage. This was crucial to his calling, since the priesthood at that time was confined only to the Levites. Accordingly, John was a priest after the order of Aaron.

Because of John's priesthood authority, Jesus sought him out when the time came for His baptism "to fulfill all righteousness" (Matthew 3:15). The Savior recognized John's priesthood authority to perform this important ordinance.

During the Apostasy, all priesthood authority was rejected and taken from the earth, requiring the fulness of the gospel to be returned. It needed to be restored. John the Baptist was sent to Joseph and Oliver in 1829 to restore the keys of the Aaronic Priesthood, of which stewardship he was custodian and caretaker.

The thirteenth section of the Doctrine and Covenants records the words of John to Joseph and Oliver on that sacred occasion:

> Upon you my fellow servants, in the name of Messiah I confer the Priesthood of Aaron, which holds the keys of the ministering of angels, and of *the gospel of repentance, and of baptism by immersion for the remission of sins;* and this shall never be taken again from the

earth, until the sons of Levi do offer again an offering unto the Lord in righteousness. (D&C 13:1)

Until the Aaronic Priesthood was restored to the earth, the keys of the gospel of repentance and of baptism for the remission of sins were absent. This means that true and complete repentance—repentance that leads to forgiveness and provides us with access to the healing powers of the Atonement—was not possible on the earth from the time of the Apostasy until May 1829. People could still make changes in their lives, quit bad habits, feel sorrow for their actions, make restitution, and exercise faith, but their sins could not be remitted and they could not be redeemed from sin until they entered into the covenant of the Atonement through baptism by one who has the authority—one who holds the Aaronic Priesthood.

Many good, obedient, faithful people looked toward Christ for their redemption during the period that the Aaronic Priesthood was gone from the earth. After all, the Light of Christ was still present. However, many of these good people recognized that the world lacked the fulness of the gospel, which inspired the great Protestant reformation that prepared the way for the eventual Restoration.

Although the Savior's portion of the Atonement had already been fulfilled, individuals on earth during the Apostasy were nevertheless in circumstances similar to those who also looked to the coming of Christ for their redemption in the times of the Old Testament. What they would have given to have the Aaronic Priesthood available to them!

In the Church today, many fail to fully appreciate and understand the significance and power of the Aaronic Priesthood. It is easy for young men who are eligible to receive the Aaronic Priesthood—and for many adults in the Church—to mistakenly diminish the significance of Aaronic Priesthood ordination. They perhaps view it as an automatic process, dependant solely upon a young man achieving a certain age. Perhaps they are troubled with the outward appearance and actions of young men who are not fully developed spiritually, and thus reason that the Aaronic Priesthood must be less meaningful if the Lord allows those young men to hold it. Those who feel so are in danger of mocking sacred things.

The Aaronic Priesthood serves, in part, to train young men so that they may honor and magnify their eventual Melchizedek Priesthood ordination and prepare for the oath and covenant that accompanies it.

But it has important sacred power by itself. The Aaronic Priesthood is more than priesthood training wheels. It holds sacred keys that unlock the power of the Atonement to man. Without these keys, the gospel cannot go forth.

As I grew up in the Church, I heard Church leaders on many occasions make statements about the power and significance of the Aaronic Priesthood. One that stuck with me was that an Aaronic Priesthood holder has more power in his little finger than all the kings, presidents, generals, and rulers that the world has ever seen. I have to admit that I wondered about that statement. How could a young man possess more power than all of these important, revered figures? How could it be true?

It is true. There is nothing that any of those leaders can do to enable anyone to obtain a remission of sins. They can do nothing to assist others in accessing the powers of the Atonement. They can do nothing to bring about sanctification, redemption, or salvation in other people's lives. They have no power to return man to God's presence. These things are controlled by heavenly powers, and the keys to these powers are held in the Aaronic Priesthood.

A sixteen-year-old priest, under the direction of his bishop, can perform baptism by immersion for the remission of sins and can administer the ordinance of the sacrament. Teachers and deacons can exercise their priesthood in the preparation and passing of the sacrament. In so doing, they provide access to the powers of the Atonement and the remission of sins. They personally represent Christ's power in performing these ordinances.

BAPTISM AS THE INITIAL ORDINANCE OF THE ATONEMENT

There was a man of the Pharisees, named Nicodemus, a ruler of the Jews:

The same came to Jesus by night, and said unto him, Rabbi, we know that thou art a teacher come from God: for no man can do these miracles that thou doest, except God be with him.

Jesus answered and said unto him, Verily, verily, I say unto thee, except a man be born again, he cannot see the kingdom of God.

Nicodemus saith unto him, how can a man be born when he is old? Can he enter the second time into his mother's womb, and be born?

> Jesus answered, Verily, verily, I say unto thee, except a man be born of water and of the Spirit, he cannot enter into the kingdom of God. (John 3:1–5)

When Jesus taught Nicodemus about the significance of baptism, He made clear that it was absolutely essential for man to return to God's presence. In other words, returning to God's presence is critical to fulfilling His purposes. If we are not baptized, we are lost.

Baptism is the initial ordinance of the Atonement, and it is performed by the authority of the Aaronic Priesthood. We are baptized for "a remission of sins," or to have our sins paid for by the Savior. The moment we enter the waters of baptism, we become partners with the Savior and establish a covenant relationship in the Atonement.

Baptism by immersion washes our sins away, and it also represents the Atonement itself. When we emerge from the water, we come forth clean and pure from the sins of the world. As we are buried by the waters of baptism and rise again, we symbolize the sacrifice, death, and Resurrection of Jesus Christ. This process also represents our own eventual resurrection, which the Savior gave as a gift to all humanity.

It is not the ritual, but the covenant of baptism that makes it irreplaceable and essential. Alma the Elder taught the covenant relationship of baptism to a "goodly number gathered together at the place of Mormon":

> And it came to pass that he said unto them: Behold, here are the waters of Mormon (for thus were they called) and now, as ye are desirous to come into the fold of God, and to be called his people, and are willing to bear one another's burdens, that they may be light;
>
> Yea, and are willing to mourn with those that mourn; yea, and comfort those that stand in need of comfort, and to stand as witnesses of God at all times and in all things, and in all places that ye may be in, even until death, that ye may be numbered with those of the first resurrection, that ye may have eternal life—
>
> Now I say unto you, if this be the desire of your hearts, what have you against being baptized in the name of the Lord, as a witness before him that ye have entered into a covenant with him, that ye will serve him and keep his commandments, that he may pour out his Spirit more abundantly upon you? (Mosiah 18:8–10)

It is no coincidence that the baptismal covenant requires that we believe, repent, pray, keep the commandments, forgive others, bear testimony of the gospel, be sincere and steadfast, and bear one another's burdens—since these are the very acts that allow us to become like Christ. Additionally, we take upon ourselves the name of Christ and promise to always remember him and live worthy of the companionship of the Holy Ghost. Simultaneously, these are also the very same conditions that the Lord requires for us to obtain forgiveness of our own sins. Combined, this is the gateway to the covenant of the Atonement.

THE SACRAMENT: THE ORDINANCE OF RENEWAL

Entering into the covenant of the Atonement with the Savior is among the most significant and solemn of all mortal decisions. The Lord treats this choice so seriously that he provides those who have been baptized the opportunity to reinforce and renew that covenant each week. We are better able to hold to our sacred promises when we receive constant reminders of them.

To active Church members, the administration of the sacrament is commonplace. But many of us do not fully contemplate the ordinance of the sacrament as we partake each week. Elder Vaughn J. Featherstone reminded us that we must not underestimate the role of the sacrament:

> Would to God that every member of this Church could understand the sacramental ordinance. Those who live the gospel from week to week, who do not commit transgressions serious enough to bring them before a common judge, have a continuous opportunity to be forgiven. All who partake of the sacrament with humble hearts and contrite spirits, who may have erred or offended during the week, can find forgiveness. Of course, repentance is also required to obtain forgiveness for each sin. Each member who renews his or her covenants through the sacrament feels the healing blessing of forgiveness. Each week we strive for a slightly loftier level of Christlike living. We need not be baptized every year or two to receive continued forgiveness. We need only approach the sacramental ordinance in a contrite, repentant, humble way in order to receive the forgiveness we desire.[1]

Jesus Christ alone wrought the great and marvelous Atonement. The ordinances and covenants associated with the Atonement are also

---

1. Vaughn J. Featherstone, *The Incomparable Christ: Our Master and Model,* (Salt Lake City: Deseret Book, 1995) 77–78.

His alone. Baptism, as the Ordinance of the Covenant, is His ordinance. So is the sacrament.

If the Savior were to appear in my ward—or yours—on a given Sunday, I believe He would do two things: first, He would minister to the children in Primary; second, He would administer His ordinance of the sacrament.

When a young man ordained as a priest in the Aaronic Priesthood officiates at the sacrament table, administering and blessing it in His name, he literally stands in for the Lord Jesus Christ. By the authority of the priesthood he holds, the priest places members of the Church under sacred covenant to remember and honor their covenant relationship with the Savior.

This ordinance of renewal is so crucial that the sacramental prayers have been revealed to us with specificity in both the Book of Mormon and the Doctrine and Covenants. These revealed prayers must be offered with exactness to ensure that their meaning is not lost or diluted. Because the sacrament serves to administer and reinforce specific covenants, the precise wording of its administration is essential—as is true of any other contract or covenant. In this sense, the sacrament prayers are not simply rote prayers; they are revealed covenants.

> It is expedient that the Church meet together often to partake of bread and wine in the remembrance of the Lord Jesus;
>
> And the elder or priest shall administer it; and after this manner shall he administer it—he shall kneel with the Church and call upon the Father in solemn prayer, saying:
>
> O God, the Eternal Father, we ask thee in the name of thy Son, Jesus Christ, to bless and sanctify this bread to the souls of all those who partake of it, that they may eat in remembrance of the body of thy Son, and witness unto thee, O God, the Eternal Father, that they are willing to take upon them the name of thy Son, and always remember him and keep his commandments which he has given them; that they may always have his Spirit to be with them. Amen.
>
> The manner of administering the wine—he shall take the cup also, and say:
>
> O God, the Eternal Father, we ask thee in the name of thy Son, Jesus Christ, to bless and sanctify this wine to the souls of all those who drink of it, that they may do it in remembrance of the blood of thy Son, which was shed for them; that they may witness unto thee,

O God, the Eternal Father, that they do always remember him, that they may have his Spirit to be with them. Amen. (D&C 20:75–79)

The sacrament is divided into two parts or emblems: the bread and the water. The sacramental prayers for each are similar but not identical. We partake of the bread in remembrance of the body of Christ; the water, in remembrance of the blood of Christ.

The bread represents the physical aspect of the atoning sacrifice. When we partake of the bread, we remember the Savior's physical suffering, humiliation, mockery, trial, crucifixion, death, and Resurrection. We are reminded of how Jesus Christ—the Bread of Life (John 6:35)—overcame physical death for all mankind and gave us the gift and promise of the Resurrection. The administration of the bread contains our commitment while in the flesh to take the name of Jesus Christ upon ourselves and become His sons and daughters.

The water represents the Savior's spiritual victory. The reference to His blood, "shed for [us]," reminds us of the tremendous spiritual suffering that the Savior endured in Gethsemane and repeated on the cross: "Which suffering caused myself, even God, the greatest of all, to tremble because of pain, and to bleed at every pore, and to suffer both body and spirit—and would that I might not drink the bitter cup, and shrink" (D&C 19:18).

While the Savior's physical suffering was indescribable, His spiritual pain was unfathomable as he struggled under the combined burden of all the sins of God's children. The administration of the sacramental water represents and remembers Christ's victory over sin, spiritual death, or eternal separation from our Heavenly Father. It is through this sacrifice that Jesus also became the fountain of living waters to the house of David and the thirsting souls of all mankind (see Joel 3:18).

As we partake, we covenant to always remember Him and to always keep His commandments. We are not required to always be perfectly obedient; we are, however, required to *try* to be perfectly obedient. As we accept these conditions, we receive His covenant to always have His Spirit to be with us. The time frame for the covenant of the sacrament is clearly for "always."

SYMBOLISM OF THE SACRAMENT

The scriptures are full of deep, rich symbolism that helps us to understand and absorb how the Savior's sacrifice for us is central to all earthly ordinances. Others have written of this symbolism with remarkable clarity:

> Throughout the scriptures, there are echoes of the symbol of water and the emblems of bread and wine that significantly direct our attention at the Atonement of Christ and our relationship with Him through participation in these symbols. Abraham shared a meal of bread and wine with Melchizedek (Genesis 14:18). In the Exodus, God's ability to give life is symbolized in the manna in the wilderness (Exodus 16:11–16), which in the Psalms becomes the "bread of angels" (Psalm 78:26), and through the water from a rock (Exodus 17:6). Under the law of Moses, each week the priests set out twelve loaves of shewbread in the temple (Leviticus 24:5–9). On the table of shewbread is a drink offering (Exodus 25:29); Numbers 4:7), probably wine. Throughout His ministry, Jesus also used these symbols to teach about the significance of His mission and the relationship between Him and His followers. He taught that baptism was being "born of water" (John 3:5) and that He was the Bread of Life (6:48). In His first miracle at Cana, Jesus turned water, stored in "waterpots of stone, after the manner of the purifying of the Jews," into wine in a story full of symbolism pointing to Jesus the Messiah fulfilling the law of Moses (2:1–11). Further, Jesus prophesied that from the belly of the Messiah would "flow rivers of living water" (7:38), which was fulfilled at least in part when the soldier pierced the side of Jesus on the cross and out came blood and water (19:34).[2]

When we partake of these emblems of Christ's physical and spiritual victories, the bread and water become part of us. As we partake of the sacrament, the bread and water become physiologically assimilated by us, and are carried in our veins to every fiber of our being. Through the covenant of the Atonement and its ordinances, Christ symbolically and literally reaches out to every part of us—always.

I believe that through the sacrament, we renew not only our baptismal covenants with the Lord, but also any other post-baptismal covenants we have entered into with Him. Baptism is a covenant of obedience, so when we renew it, all of the subsequent covenants that we have entered into are inherently included. Since every covenant gives us

---

2. David Roth Seely, ed. by Richard Neitzel Holzapfel and Thomas A. Wayment, *From the Last Supper through the Resurrection: The Savior's Final Hours*, (Salt Lake City: Deseret Book, 2003) 95.

additional endowments of blessings, promises, knowledge, and powers of the Atonement—bringing us closer to our Savior—the emblems of the sacrament serve to renew all covenants we have made. Others share this opinion: "Of the edification-type ordinances, the sacrament service comes the closest to being a salvation-type ordinance, both because of its symbolic representation of Christ's Atonement and also because it renews the covenant of the baptism *and temple vows*."[3]

If this principle is true, it strongly suggests a connection between the Atonement and the enabling power the Atonement provides for us to receive further, additional blessings by covenant. It teaches us by symbolic means that it is through the atoning powers of the sacrifice of Jesus Christ that the blessings of the temple are made available to us. To me, this doctrine certainly rings true. I believe that members who have been endowed also renew their temple covenants through the sacrament. Perhaps also, Melchizedek Priesthood holders renew the covenant by which the priesthood is received. Marriage covenants in which the Lord is a partner may also be included. Conceivably, even personal and private covenants between ourselves and our Savior are renewed.

King Benjamin taught his people the significance of making such all-encompassing "righteous covenants" with the Savior:

> There is no other name given whereby salvation cometh; there-fore, I would that ye should take upon you the name of Christ, all you that have entered into the covenant with God that ye should be obedient unto the end of your lives.
>
> And it shall come to pass that whosoever doeth this shall be found at the right hand of God, for he shall know the name by which he is called; for he shall be called by the name of Christ.
>
> And now it shall come to pass, that whosoever shall not take upon him the name of Christ must be called by some other name; therefore, he findeth himself on the left hand of God.
>
> And I would that ye should remember also, that this is the name that I said I should give unto you that never should be blotted out, except it be through transgression; therefore, take heed that ye do not transgress, that the name be not blotted out of your hearts.
>
> I say unto you, I would that ye should remember to retain the

---

3. Victor L. Ludlow, *Principles and Practices of the Restored Gospel*, (Salt Lake City: Deseret Book, 1992) 349; emphasis added.

name written always in your hearts, that ye are not found on the left hand of God, but that ye hear and know the voice by which ye shall be called, and also, the name by which he shall call you. (Mosiah 5:8–12)

Those who enter into and honor these covenants take upon themselves the name of Christ. They are accepted of him if they "retain the name written always in [their] hearts." They do not doubt to whom they belong; they know the name by which they are called.

The sacrament, that ordinance of renewal, qualifies us to be accepted of the Savior and to be called by His name each week. Through partaking of the sacrament, obeying commandments, and repenting, we are cleansed of sin. We receive the promise of the sanctifying power of the Holy Ghost, and we are reminded of our sacred obligations of remembrance. If we are worthy partakers, we are forgiven and sanctified, and "we may have this hope; that we may be purified even as he is pure" (Moroni 7:48).

CHAPTER FOUR

The New and Everlasting Covenant

And the Father teacheth him of the covenant which he has renewed and confirmed upon you, which is confirmed upon you for your sakes, and not for your sakes only, but for the sake of the whole world.

—Doctrine and Covenants 84:48

COVENANTS ARE INTEGRAL TO THE GOSPEL OF JESUS Christ. Through covenants, our Heavenly Father instructs us, gives us hope, blesses our lives, and obtains our commitment to Him. As we grow in the gospel, our Heavenly Father's plan leads us "line upon line, precept upon precept," and covenant upon covenant along a pathway back to His presence.

The definition and origin of the word *covenant* is instructive. As a noun, it denotes a solemn agreement, a contract, and an agreement held as the basis for a commitment with God. As a verb, it is used to indicate payment by covenant.

But one meaning of the Hebrew root for the word *covenant* is "to choose" or "to select." This suggests that it is through the use of covenants that God selects His "covenant people" from among all of His children, thus forming "a chosen generation, a royal priesthood, an holy nation, a peculiar people" (1 Peter 2:9). We are not "peculiar" to the Lord in the sense of being odd or strange. Instead, we are peculiar in the sense that we are uniquely His; we are cherished and treasured, having been "bought with a price" (1 Corinthians 6:20). As His people, we properly bear His name, through the ordinances of the Aaronic Priesthood when we covenant that we "are willing to take upon [us] the name of thy Son" (D&C 20:77).

However, this selection process is not accomplished arbitrarily. It is, instead, divinely designed so that He accepts all those who faithfully choose to come unto Him, to obey Him, and to commit to Him. By covenant, He chooses those who choose Him. Remember, His sheep hear His voice (see John 10:27).

The origin of the word *covenant* comes from the Latin verb *convenire*, which means "to come together," "to make one," or in other words, "to become at-one." Indeed, it can be said that the basis, meaning, and concepts of the words *covenant* and *atonement* are very similar. Doctrinally, the covenant cannot exist without the Atonement, and the Atonement cannot exist without the covenant.

As members of The Church of Jesus Christ of Latter-day Saints, we make a multitude of covenants that may, at first, seem unrelated. We know that each covenant serves its own unique purpose, but it is often difficult to understand how they are all related. Elder Russell M. Nelson helps us understand that the covenants of the gospel of Jesus Christ are inherently connected and cohesive in nature:

> In short, *all covenants*, all testaments, all holy witnesses since the beginning *have essentially been about one thing—the Atonement of Jesus Christ*, the at-one-ment provided every man, woman, and child if they will but receive the witness. The testimony of the prophets and apostles, and honor the terms of that coming together, that convenire, or covenant, whose central feature is always the atoning sacrifice of the Son of God himself.[1]

We readily associate many gospel milestones with specific covenants. For example, we are generally familiar with the covenants associated with baptism, the sacrament, the priesthood, the temple endowment, and eternal marriage. We know of the covenant God made with Abraham which continues to have such a tremendous impact not only on the world's events in these last days but also on the hearts of individuals. But other covenants exist as well. For example, Elder Jeffrey R. Holland has eloquently explained in his book, *Christ and the New Covenant*, that the Book of Mormon is received as God's "new covenant" to the children of Israel.

Each of these covenants, taken separately, is significant and sacred,

---

1. Jeffrey R. Holland, *Christ and the New Covenant*, (Salt Lake City: Deseret Book, 1997) 8; emphasis added.

but I have personally come to believe, as Elder Nelson implies, that all of these covenants are appendages to one great, infinite, and eternal covenant: the Atonement of Jesus Christ. President John Taylor said, "A covenant was entered into between [Jesus] and His Father, in which He agreed to atone for the sins of the world; and He thus, as stated, became the Lamb slain from before the foundation of the world."[2]

We know from the books of Abraham and Moses that Jesus was foreordained to be the Christ, our Savior and Messiah. His foreordination was the pinnacle of the premortal experience for God's children. President Taylor tells us that Jesus entered into a covenant there "in which He agreed to atone for the sins of the world." The Prophet Joseph Smith taught that this everlasting covenant included all three members of the Godhead: "[The] Everlasting Covenant was made *between three personages before the organization of this earth,* and relates to their dispensation of things to men on the earth; these personages, according to Abraham's record, are called God the first, the Creator; God the second, the Redeemer; and God the third, the witness or Testator."[3]

This infinite Atonement is the infinite covenant. The infinite covenant, often called the everlasting covenant—pertaining to the "work and glory" of God in bringing to pass the "exaltation and eternal life of man" (Moses 1:39)—encompasses each of the covenants that we make in our progression. The separate covenants of the gospel are not independent of the Atonement and have little value without the atoning sacrifice of Jesus Christ. The Atonement fulfills each covenant we make with our Father in Heaven. The Atonement is the reward for all the promises God makes to man.

Thus, our willing participation in each of these seemingly divergent gospel covenants ties our hearts and desires to the Savior and His atoning powers. The Atonement of Jesus Christ and the gospel of repentance, which teaches us to access those sacred powers, is the essence of the everlasting covenant. As President Joseph Fielding Smith wrote: "Now there is a clear-cut definition in detail of the new and everlasting covenant. *It is everything—the fulness of the gospel.* So marriage properly performed, baptism, ordination to the priesthood,

---

2.   John Taylor, *Mediation and Atonement,* (1882) 96–97.

3.   Joseph Smith, *Teachings of the Prophet Joseph Smith,* Selected by Joseph Fielding Smith, (Salt Lake City: Deseret Book, 1976) 190; emphasis added.

everything else—every contract, every obligation, *every performance that pertains to the gospel of Jesus Christ, which is sealed by the Holy Spirit of promise* according to his law here given, *is part of the new and everlasting covenant.*"[4]

AN INFINITE AND ETERNAL ATONEMENT

In the land of Gideon, Alma taught: "For behold, I say unto you there be many things to come; and behold, there is one thing which is of more importance than they all—for behold, the time is not far distant that the Redeemer liveth and cometh among his people" (Alma 7:7).

The Atonement of Jesus Christ is the singular, central act of all eternity. It overshadows all of the acts of all the inhabitants of all of the worlds created by the hand of God. When the Lord spoke to Moses about His purposes, He hinted concerning His infinite creations: "The heavens, they are many, and *they cannot be numbered unto man;* but they are numbered unto me, for they are mine. And as one earth shall pass away, and the heavens thereof even so shall another come, and *there is no end to my works,* neither to my words. For behold, this is my work and my glory—to bring to pass the immortality and eternal life of man" (Moses 1:37–39, emphasis added).

The infinite and ongoing "work and glory" of the Lord, then, is to perfect us so that we can live eternally in His presence. This is why our world, and other "worlds without number," have been created. The earth is a proving ground, as described in the Pearl of Great Price: "And *we will prove them herewith,* to see if they will do all things whatsoever the Lord their God shall command them; And they who keep their first estate shall be added upon; and they who keep not their first estate shall not have glory in the same kingdom with those who keep their first estate; and they who keep their second estate shall have glory added upon their heads for ever and ever" (Abraham 3:25–26, emphasis added).

Yet this proving process involves incredible risk. For each of us—with the sole exception of Jesus Christ—sin is inevitable. That reality assures us that there will be serious consequence to our sins. Once tainted, we cannot return to God's presence. Sin renders us unclean and unqualified to be in His presence and glory. "Wherefore, if ye

---

4.   Joseph Fielding Smith, *Doctrines of Salvation,* 1:158.

have sought to do wickedly in the days of your probation, then ye are found unclean before the judgment-seat of God; and *no unclean thing can dwell with God;* wherefore, ye must be cast off forever" (1 Nephi 10:21, emphasis added).

The Atonement of Jesus Christ is the most significant and sacred event of all eternity because it prevents the entire human family from being cast out as a consequence of sin. Without it, the very purposes of our Heavenly Father would fail, for we could achieve neither immortality nor eternal life. Without the Atonement, God would cease to be God.

The infinite and eternal nature of our Heavenly Father's purposes and creations requires an equally infinite and eternal atonement. For sinners to be reconciled to God, and to have every trace of sin erased, there must be an atonement. An infinite and eternal sacrifice must be offered to meet the demands of justice, requiring the price for sin be paid; however, that same sacrifice must also offer mercy to those who have sinned.

This was the purpose of Christ's mission. As the Only Begotten of the Father in the flesh, Christ alone possessed the power and authority to lay down His life and take it up again. He, alone, lived a perfect, sinless life. He, alone, was qualified to make the required infinite sacrifice. The Creator of "worlds without number" was required to make a personal sacrifice that was without limits, a sacrifice that would impact His entire, infinite creation. The scriptures teach this also:

> And after they have been scattered, and the Lord God hath scourged them by other nations for the space of many generations, yea, even down from generation to generation until they shall be persuaded to believe in Christ, the Son of God, and the Atonement, which is infinite for all mankind—and when that day shall come that they shall believe in Christ, and worship the Father in his name, with pure hearts and clean hands, and look not forward any more for another Messiah, then, at that time, the day will come that it must needs be expedient that they should believe these things. (2 Nephi 25:16)

> That by him, and through him, and of him, the worlds are and were created, and the inhabitants thereof are begotten sons and daughters unto God. (D&C 76:24)

THE CENTRAL DOCTRINE OF ALL COVENANTS

Throughout time, all things taught by inspiration have pointed us to the Atonement. Long before the birth of Jesus, the teachings of the prophets were designed to direct the people toward the coming of the Savior. The law of Moses, for example, was given specifically to prepare the people to receive the Messiah. Nephi and Alma wrote:

> For we labor diligently to write, to persuade our children, and also our brethren, to believe in Christ, and to be reconciled to God; for we know that it is by grace that we are saved, after all we can do.
>
> And, *notwithstanding we believe in Christ, we keep the law of Moses, and look forward with steadfastness unto Christ, until the law shall be fulfilled.*
>
> *For, for this end was the law given; wherefore the law hath become dead unto us, and we are made alive in Christ because of our faith;* yet we keep the law because of the commandments.
>
> And *we talk of Christ, we rejoice in Christ, we preach of Christ, we prophesy of Christ,* and we write according to our prophecies, that our children may know to what source they may look for a remission of their sins.
>
> Wherefore, we speak concerning the law that our children may know *the deadness of the law;* and they, by knowing the deadness of the law, may look forward unto that life which is in Christ, and *know for what end the law was given.* And after the law is fulfilled in Christ, that they *need not harden their hearts against him when the law ought to be done away.* (2 Nephi 25:23–27, emphasis added)

> And behold, this is the whole meaning of the law, every whit pointing to that great and last sacrifice; and that great and last sacrifice will be the Son of God, yea, infinite and eternal. (Alma 34:14)

An infinite atonement, operative throughout all time, space, and creation, is only accessible to us by a specific, infinite covenant. Yet, we may still tend to think of our covenants in the plural sense. We have been taught about baptismal and post-baptismal covenants into which we must enter to receive exaltation, as if they are all separate and independent. Perhaps it is more correct to understand that all covenants required of us by our Heavenly Father are appendages to the single, central covenant of the Atonement of Jesus Christ—the everlasting covenant.

The gospel is the everlasting covenant because it is ordained by Him who is Everlasting and also because it is everlastingly the same. In all past ages salvation was gained by adherence to its terms and conditions, and that same compliance will bring the same reward in all future ages. Each time this everlasting covenant is revealed it is new to those of that dispensation. Hence the gospel is the new and everlasting covenant. *All covenants between God and man are part of the new and everlasting covenant.*[5]

We can safely deduce from the teachings of Joseph Smith, John Taylor, and Elder McConkie that the covenant pertaining to the Atonement is the essence of the new and everlasting covenant and that all other covenants are designed to give us additional access to the blessings of the Savior's sacrifice. The scriptures repeatedly teach this principle.

The Doctrine and Covenants reveals that the everlasting covenant was established "from the beginning" (D&C 22:1, 49:9). The scriptures teach that this everlasting covenant is mediated by Jesus Christ (see Hebrews 12:24), "through the shedding of his own blood" (D&C 76:69), and that the everlasting covenant is sent "into the world, to be a light to the world, and to be a standard for my people" (D&C 45:9).

Joseph Fielding Smith wrote that the everlasting covenant "is the promise of God to grant to man, through man's obedience and acceptance of the ordinances and principles of the gospel, *the glory and exaltation of eternal life.*"[6] It is not a stretch to say that the "glory and exaltation of eternal life" is brought about directly through the Atonement. This definition establishes a correlation between the Atonement and the temple covenants. Covenants made in the temple bring promises of exaltation which go far beyond the blessings promised at baptism.

With that perspective, President Smith instructs:

What is the new and everlasting covenant? I regret to say that there are some members of the Church who are misled and misinformed in regard to what the new and everlasting covenant really is. The new and everlasting covenant is the sum total of all gospel covenants and obligations, and I want to prove it. In the sixty-sixth

---

5. McConkie, *Mormon Doctrine*, 529–530; emphasis added.
6. Joseph Fielding Smith, *Doctrines of Salvation*, compiled by Bruce R. McConkie, vol. 1, (Salt Lake City: Bookcraft, 1954–56) 152; emphasis added.

section of the Doctrine and Covenants, verse two, I read: "Verily I say unto you, blessed are you for receiving *mine everlasting covenant, even the fulness of my gospel,* sent forth unto the children of men, *that they might have life* and *be made partakers of the glories* which are to be revealed in the last days, as it was written by the prophets and apostles in days of old."[7]

Through Christ's sacrifice, we are given access to not only the cleansing powers of forgiveness through the waters of baptism but also the fulness of the glories of God: "Therefore all that my Father hath shall be given unto him" (D&C 84:38).

COME UNTO CHRIST

In the simplest terms, the gospel message—of which the Atonement is the centerpiece—is the plea to "come unto Christ," because that is the only way to access the Atonement. The Book of Mormon prophet, Amaleki, taught that coming to Christ is not something that can be accomplished without total and complete commitment: "And now, my beloved brethren, I would that ye should *come unto Christ,* who is the Holy One of Israel, and partake of his salvation, and the power of his redemption. Yea, come unto him, and *offer your whole souls* as an offering unto him, and continue in fasting and praying, and endure to the end; and as the Lord liveth ye will be saved" (Omni 1:26, emphasis added).

Through faith, repentance, and baptism we accept Jesus Christ as our Savior and Redeemer. By covenant, we take upon ourselves the name of Christ and become known as Christians and Saints. We offer our "whole souls" to Him by our willing obedience.

King Benjamin taught that those who accept Christ's Atonement, commandments, and gospel teachings establish another type of relationship with the Savior. We become born of him: "And now, because of the covenant which ye have made ye shall be called the children of Christ, his sons, and his daughters; for behold, this day *he hath spiritually begotten you;* for ye say that your hearts are changed through faith on his name; therefore, *ye are born of him and have become his sons and his daughters*" (Mosiah 5:7, emphasis added).

As Christ's sons and daughters, we are implicitly and symbolically

---

7. Smith, *Doctrines of Salvation,* 1:156; emphasis added.

taught that we have the potential to become like Him. Indeed, Moroni taught that the ultimate end result of coming to Christ is to become like Him. "Wherefore, my beloved brethren, pray unto the Father with all the energy of heart, that ye may be filled with this love, which he hath bestowed upon all who are true followers of his Son, Jesus Christ; that ye may become the sons of God; that when he shall appear *we shall be like him,* for we shall see him as he is; *that we may have this hope; that we may be purified even as he is pure.* Amen" (Moroni 7:48, emphasis added).

This happens as we receive, grace by grace, the additional blessings and powers that the Atonement of Jesus Christ offers us through our entering into post-baptismal covenants that access additional atoning powers.

THE MESSENGER OF THE COVENANT

Malachi's words have had such significance to our Heavenly Father's children that he was directly quoted not only by the resurrected Savior when speaking to the Nephites but also by the angel Moroni when he instructed Joseph Smith preceding the Restoration of the gospel of Jesus Christ on the earth (see JS–H 1:36):

> And it came to pass that he commanded them that they should write the words which the Father had given unto Malachi, which he should tell unto them. And it came to pass that after they were written he expounded them. And these are the words which he did tell unto them, saying: Thus said the Father unto Malachi—Behold, I will send my messenger, and he shall prepare the way before me, and the Lord whom ye seek shall suddenly come to his temple, *even the messenger of the covenant,* whom ye delight in; behold, he shall come, saith the Lord of Hosts. (3 Nephi 24:1, emphasis added)

The Savior reminded the Nephites of events that accompany the establishment—or reestablishment—of the covenant on the earth: the Lord will "suddenly come to his temple." That prophesy has been partially fulfilled on at least two occasions: first, when the resurrected Christ appeared at the temple in the land Bountiful as recorded in the Book of Mormon, and; second, when the Lord came suddenly to His temple on April 3, 1836 as described in the one hundred tenth section of the Doctrine and Covenants.

In these events—as well as in any subsequent temple appearances that will complete the fulfillment of this prophesy—the Savior is identified by Malachi, notably, as the "messenger of the covenant." Jesus made it clear throughout His ministry that He was not on His own errand. He repeatedly emphasized that He had been sent from the Father; he was the messenger of the covenant spoken of by Malachi.

> And he said unto them, I must preach the kingdom of God to other cities also: for therefore am I sent. (Luke 4:43)

> But I have greater witness than that of John: for the works which the Father hath given me to finish, the same works that I do, bear witness of me, that the Father hath sent me. (John 5:36)

> As the living Father hath sent me, and I live by the Father: so he that eateth me, even he shall live by me. (John 6:57)

> But I know him: for I am from him, and he hath sent me. (John 7:29)

> Jesus said unto them, If God were your Father, ye would love me: for I proceeded forth and came from God; neither came I of myself, but he sent me. (John 8:42)

> Say ye of him, whom the Father hath sanctified, and sent into the world, Thou blasphemest; because I said, I am the Son of God? (John 10:36)

> And I knew that thou hearest me always: but because of the people that stand by I said it, that they may believe that thou has sent me. (John 11:42)

> And this is life eternal, that they might know thee the only true God, and Jesus Christ, whom thou hast sent. (John 17:3)

The question may be raised, of which covenant was Jesus sent as the messenger? Was it the covenant of the law of Moses? Of Abraham? Of Noah? Of John?

He was and is the messenger of all these, which are but one covenant of salvation through the Atonement. Jesus Christ was sent from the Father as the messenger of the infinite covenant of the Atonement, which spans and encompasses all dispensations.

THE MASTER OF THE COVENANT

The purpose of the new and everlasting covenant—the covenant of the Atonement—is to make us like our Savior. It is to purify us, sanctify us, perfect us, and exalt us. This is the very essence of eternal life.

It is instructive to note that one title for Jesus Christ is Master. The term *master* has several meanings. Significantly, one modern meaning of the term is an original from which duplicates can be made. Christ, as the Master of the covenant, provides us with not only the perfect example for our lives but also offers Himself by covenant to make us as He is.

The fulfillment of the covenant involves different parties in different stages at different times. Again, as President Taylor said, Jesus entered into His portion of the covenant "before the foundation of the world." Then, in the Garden of Gethsemane, on the cross of Golgotha, and in arising from the tomb, Jesus fulfilled His portion of the covenant by taking upon Himself the sins of the world and overcoming death. He willingly did so, offering His body and His blood to seal the covenant.

For us, we enter into the covenant in steps, for we are instructed "line upon line; here a little, and there a little" (Isaiah 28:10). Indeed, we are not capable of entering into the fulness of the covenant all at once. Only as we live principles we have already received are we able to grow sufficiently to be able to receive the principles, ordinances, and covenants that come next. We are not equipped to enter into the full covenant without significant work, effort, and spiritual growth. Individual responsibility and accountability is added upon us each step of the way. Christ does not require us to enter into the full covenant spiritually (or otherwise) immature, lest we be held eternally accountable and responsible for sacred things for which we are not prepared.

Initially, through the gate of baptism, we demonstrate faith unto repentance. In so doing, we become parties to the covenant. We establish a covenant relationship with our Savior that allows us to be forgiven and our sins remitted under conditions of repentance. However, being forgiven does not necessarily or automatically lead us to perfection or exaltation. Obtaining forgiveness at some point in our lives may or may not save us from our past sins—depending upon our ability to endure to the end—but it certainly does not save us from our future sins. Forgiveness alone, then, does not fulfill the purpose of the Atonement to make us like He is. There is yet more.

So, at appropriate times, as we spiritually mature and our capacities and understanding increase, we are asked to enter into additional covenants. These covenants, required of the house of Israel—including, for all of God's sons, the receipt of the Melchizedek Priesthood and, for all of God's children, those covenants entered into in the House of the Lord—endow us with knowledge and power that allow us to follow the example of our Master and become like Him in all things.

These additional covenants are not separate from the Atonement of Jesus any more than the office of deacon is separate from the priesthood. These covenants are integral to our receiving the full blessings offered to man through the Atonement. Combined, all of these covenants are the divine process by which we truly become at-one with our Savior and Heavenly Father. These additional covenants add to our understanding of the Atonement and give us additional access to its sanctifying, healing, exalting, and sealing powers.

FORGIVENESS AND THE REMISSION OF SINS

In order to repent and obtain forgiveness, it is critical to understand and have faith in the centerpiece of the new and everlasting covenant: the Atonement. It is only through the power of the Atonement that our sins can be forgiven, or remitted.

To remit means "to pay for." In the context of sin, remittance is made and sin is paid for only through suffering. There is no other way.

> For behold, I, God, have suffered these things for all, that they might not suffer if they would repent;
> But if they would not repent they must suffer even as I;
> Which suffering caused myself, even God, the greatest of all to tremble because of pain, and to bleed at every pore, and to suffer both body and spirit—and would that I might not drink the bitter cup and shrink—Nevertheless, glory be to the Father, and I partook and finished my preparations unto the children of men. (D&C 19:16–19)

This scripture paints a vivid mental image in my mind of our Savior, kneeling in agony and pain, "how sore you know not, how exquisite you know not, yea, how hard to bear you know not" (D&C 19:15), bleeding from every pore in the Garden of Gethsemane and hanging on the cross at Golgotha. What a price was paid for us!

We may never completely comprehend how He did it, but He did! He suffered the weight and consequences for our sins, He felt all the pain that we have ever inflicted upon others as a result of our actions.

He also suffered all of the pain and hurt that others have inflicted upon us. In so doing, the demands of justice for sin have been paid. "For ye are bought with a price: therefore glorify God in your body, and in your spirit, which are God's" (1 Corinthians 6:20).

Christ paid for our sins, whether we repent of them or not. As a result, He alone has the right to set conditions that are required for obtaining forgiveness. Here are a few of the requirements:

> Nevertheless, he that repents and *does the commandments of the Lord* shall be forgiven. (D&C 1:32, emphasis added)

> *Judge not*, and ye shall not be judged: *condemn not*, and ye shall not be condemned: *forgive*, and ye shall be forgiven. (Luke 6:37, emphasis added)

> And it came to pass that I did frankly forgive them all that they had done, and I did exhort them that they would *pray unto the Lord their God for forgiveness.* And it came to pass that they did so. (1 Nephi 7:21, emphasis added)

> Therefore I say unto you, Go; and whosoever transgresseth against me, him shall ye judge according to the sins which he has committed; and if he *confess his sins before thee and me*, and *repenteth in the sincerity of his heart*, him shall ye forgive, and I will forgive him also. (Mosiah 26:29, emphasis added)

> Therefore, *thrust in your sickle with all your soul*, and your sins are forgiven you, and you shall be laden with sheaves upon your back, for the laborer is worthy of his hire. (D&C 31:5, emphasis added)

> For I will forgive you of your sins with this commandment— that you *remain steadfast in your minds in solemnity and the spirit of prayer*, in *bearing testimony to all the world* of those things which are communicated unto you. (D&C 84:61, emphasis added)

> For behold, this is my church; whosoever is baptized shall *be baptized unto repentance.* And whomsoever ye receive shall *believe in my name*; and him will I freely forgive. (Mosiah 26:22, emphasis added)

Believe. Repent. Pray. Keep the commandments. Forgive others. Bear testimony of the gospel. Be sincere. Be steadfast. These are some of the conditions upon which forgiveness can be received.

A Place within His Heart

But this is not all. We are required to do all of these things by covenant. That is, we must enter into the new and everlasting covenant. Without a willingness to enter into the covenant by accepting these terms through baptism, we live beyond the power of the Atonement. As the words of the sacrament hymn teach us, sung by those who have made that sacred commitment, only after we become a party to the covenant do we have a part in His offering:

> Oh, love effulgent, love divine!
> What debt of gratitude is mine,
> That in His offering I have part,
> And hold a place within His heart.[8]

When we accept His terms and conditions, we do have a part in the Atonement—but not until then. By accepting these terms and conditions through baptism, our relationship with the Savior and access to His sacrifice is different than it was before we committed ourselves by covenant. We gain special rights and privileges that never existed before. Jesus Christ becomes our specific and personal Savior and Redeemer, rather than merely a general and theoretical one. Baptism establishes a sacred relationship with Him, which otherwise would not be present.

Perfection

When Joseph Smith and Sidney Rigdon received a vision of the three degrees of glory, they saw the celestial kingdom and its inhabitants. There, they saw the ultimate result of just men and women who have had a part in Christ's offering. These, the scriptures say, were "made perfect" and received a fulness of all of God's promises to His children. "These are they who are *just men made perfect through Jesus the Mediator of the new covenant*, who wrought out this perfect atonement through the shedding of his own blood" (D&C 76:69, emphasis added).

To be made perfect strongly implies that these just men had fulfilled Christ's directives to both the Jews in Jerusalem and the Nephites in the Book of Mormon: "Be ye therefore perfect." In that context, perfection means far more than simply having had sins remitted, however.

---

8. "God Loved Us, So He Sent His Son," *Hymns,* 187.

Prior to His experience in the crucible of the Atonement, Jesus said that their example of perfection was the Father: "Be ye therefore perfect, even as your Father which is in heaven is perfect" (Matthew 5:48).

Though He lived a perfect and sinless life, the Savior did not use himself as an example of this type of perfection. He lacked one important thing: He had not yet been exalted and had not yet become like unto the Father. After His death and Resurrection, however, that exaltation had been attained. Hence, Jesus told the Nephites that their perfection should model not only the Father's but His perfection also: "Therefore, I would that ye should be perfect even as I, or your Father who is in heaven is perfect" (3 Nephi 12:48).

Of the two specified elements of the work and glory of God, then, the Resurrection and remission of sins provides only for immortality in full. Eternal life requires somewhat more.

EXALTATION AND THE EVERLASTING COVENANT

The concept of eternal life is one of those principles to which the scriptures apply layered meanings. At one level, the term *eternal life* is closely associated with immortality: Christ's victory over the grave, thus providing the gift of the Resurrection to all men. Paul taught this concept in Corinth when he told them that "in Christ shall all be made alive" (1 Corinthians 15:22). This is consistent with what the disciples understood when Jesus, immediately before raising Lazarus from the dead, said: "I am the resurrection *and the life:* he that believeth in me, though he were dead, *yet shall he live:* And whosoever liveth and believeth in me *shall never die*" (John 11:25–26).

However, true eternal life encompasses more than simply living forever; it also refers to a specific type of living—a celestial quality of life, if you will. Elder Bruce R. McConkie taught, "Celestial marriage is the gate to exaltation, and exaltation consists in the continuation of the family unit in eternity. Exaltation is eternal life, the kind of life which God lives. Those who obtain it gain an inheritance in the highest of the three heavens within the celestial kingdom."[9]

At this other level, eternal life refers, as Elder McConkie said, to "the kind of life which God lives." From this context, the concept of eternal life imputes all of the power, knowledge, wisdom, righteousness,

---

9.   McConkie, *Mormon Doctrine*, 257.

understanding, intelligence, and glory that belong to God. It takes on this usage from one of the very names of God. "Behold, I am God; Man of Holiness is my name; Man of Counsel is my name; and *Endless and Eternal is my name, also.* Wherefore, I can stretch forth mine hands and hold all the creations which I have made; and mine eye can pierce them also" (Moses 7:35–36, emphasis added).

President Joseph Fielding Smith wrote directly on the topic of this distinction between immortality and eternal life: "Immortality and eternal life are two separate things, one distinct from the other. Every man shall receive immortality, whether he be good, bad or indifferent, for the Resurrection from the dead shall come to all. Eternal life is something in addition."[10]

While baptism is the gate for salvation and the remission of sins, it is significant to understand that baptism is only one of several necessary and essential gates for exaltation and eternal life. Salvation and eternal life/exaltation are two different dimensions to God's work and glory. The requirements for salvation are not necessarily the same as the requirements for exaltation and eternal life. Through the blessings of salvation, virtually all of God's children are ensured of a resurrection to some varying degree of glory.

On the one hand, immortality to just any degree of eternal glory is a free gift to those who kept their first estate by coming to earth and who avoid becoming a son of perdition while here. On the other hand, obtaining eternal life requires covenants. Although we are salvaged from eternal uselessness by a remission of our sins, faith, repentance, and baptism, and we enter into the covenant of the Atonement through baptism, additional covenants on our part are necessary for us to enter into and keep for exaltation to be attained. These covenants open additional access to the powers of the covenant of the Atonement in our lives: powers to make us as He is.

In the vision Joseph Smith and Sidney Rigdon received of the degrees of glory, recorded in the seventy-sixth section of the Doctrine and Covenants, we read about those who have accessed the powers of the everlasting covenant—the covenant of the Atonement—to become cleansed, sanctified, purified, enlightened, empowered, glorified, and endowed. They have attained these attributes—which are collectively attributes of godhood—as they kept the commandments, received

---

10. Smith, *Doctrines of Salvation,* 2:4.

greater light and knowledge, and have entered into the various covenants that have led them down the pathway to exaltation:

> And again, we bear record—for we saw and heard, and this is the testimony of the gospel of Christ concerning them *who shall come forth in the resurrection of the just*—
>
> They are they who *received the testimony of Jesus*, and *believed on his name* and *were baptized* after the manner of his burial, being buried in water in his name, and this according to the commandment which he has given—
>
> That by *keeping the commandments* they might be washed and cleansed from all their sins, and *receive the Holy Spirit* by the laying on of the hands of him who is ordained and s*ealed unto this power;* and who overcome by *faith*, and are *sealed by the Holy Spirit of promise*, which the Father sheds forth upon all those who are just and true.
>
> They are they who are the Church of the Firstborn.
>
> *They are they into whose hands the Father has given all things*—
>
> They are they who are *priests and kings*, who have received of his fulness, and of his glory;
>
> *And are priests of the Most High, after the order of Melchizedek,* which was after the order of Enoch, which was after the order of the Only Begotten Son. Wherefore, as it is written, *they are gods, even the sons of God*—
>
> Wherefore *all things are theirs*, whether life or death, or things present, or things to come, all are theirs and they are Christ's and Christ is God's.
>
> And they shall overcome all things. (D&C 76:50–60, emphasis added)

The blessing of receiving "all things" from the Father is available to all who add upon their baptismal covenant through obedience and additional priesthood covenants and ordinances. A man may have "entered in by the way" (2 Nephi 32:1) through the waters of baptism; he may have gained a remission of his sins through repentance; he may have a testimony of the Savior; he may keep the commandments; he may receive the Holy Ghost. He may do all of these things and not attain exaltation, unless he continues to come unto Christ through the other, additional covenants that God has provided for that purpose. He must enter into sacred covenants in the House of the Lord. Worthy brethren are required to also receive the priesthood by oath and covenant. Access to the priesthood and the temple are made possible to man through the atoning sacrifice. Further, the temple is the location designated by the Lord where access to these additional blessings are made available to all who have ever lived on the earth—all of which is made possible by Christ's atoning sacrifice.

> For whoso is faithful unto the obtaining these two priesthoods of which I have spoken, and the magnifying their calling, are sanctified by the Spirit unto the renewing of their bodies.
>
> They become the sons of Moses and of Aaron and the seed of Abraham, and the Church and kingdom and the elect of God.
>
> And also *all they who receive this priesthood receive me*, saith the Lord;
>
> For he that receiveth my servants receiveth me;
>
> And he that receiveth me receiveth my Father;
>
> And he that receiveth my Father receiveth my Father's kingdom, *therefore all that my Father hath shall be given unto him.*
>
> And this is according to the oath and covenant which belongeth to the priesthood. (D&C 84:33–39, emphasis added)

They have eternal increase, a continuation of the seeds forever and ever, a continuation of the lives, eternal lives; that is, they have spirit children in the resurrection, in relation to which offspring they stand in the same position that God our Father stands to us. They inherit in due course the fulness of the glory of the Father, meaning that they have all power in heaven and on earth (see D&C 76:50–60, 93:1–40). "*Then shall they be gods*, because they have no end; therefore shall they be from everlasting to everlasting, because they continue; then shall they be above all, because all things are subject unto them. *Then shall they be gods, because they have all power,* and the angels are subject unto them."[11]

"In the celestial glory there are three heavens or degrees; And in order to obtain the highest, a man must enter into this order of the priesthood (meaning the new and everlasting covenant of marriage); And if he does not, he cannot obtain it. He may enter into the other, but that is the end of his kingdom; he cannot have an increase" (D&C 131:1–4). Can a man receive all the Father has without becoming one with Him? Is it possible for man to humbly and obediently approach the throne of heaven seeking the mercies of God in the blessings of exaltation without becoming perfected? Is perfection possible on our

---

11. McConkie, *Mormon Doctrine*, 257.

own? Can a man become like unto God without becoming at-one with the traits, characteristics, qualities and attributes of godhood? The answer is very clear: No!

Thus, exaltation and eternal life are the ultimate expression and fulfillment of the covenant which was from the beginning. This everlasting covenant, made by and between the members of the Godhead before the world was, is made available to us through the infinite, atoning sacrifice of Jesus Christ. We are exalted through the fulness of the new and everlasting covenant: the Atonement wrought by Jesus Christ and the plan of salvation and redemption that He made possible.

THE HOLY GHOST: A BLESSING OF THE COVENANT

One who has gained entrance into the new and everlasting covenant through the waters of baptism then receives the gift of the Holy Ghost by the laying on of hands. This is the precious, sanctifying, inestimable blessing that follows the covenant. The guidance and influence of the Holy Ghost assists those who have part in the covenant with avoiding sin, leading them to additional covenants and confirming the Savior's acceptance of a life righteously lived.

Also known as the Comforter, the Holy Ghost's primary role is to testify of truth. It is by the influence of the Holy Ghost that a testimony of Jesus Christ as the Messiah, Savior, and Redeemer is obtained. It is through the Holy Ghost that a testimony of the divinity of the Book of Mormon and the Prophet Joseph Smith is received. He bears witness of the truth and reality of the very covenants we take upon ourselves. The witness of the Holy Ghost binds us to these covenants and reminds us of them as the sacramental prayer promises; "that [we] may always have his Spirit to be with [us]." He testifies of all truth, in any form, wherever it is found.

Significantly, the Holy Ghost also sanctifies the receiver. Understanding this sacred role of the Holy Ghost is important in the process of obtaining forgiveness. As the Savior taught the Nephites: "Now this is the commandment: Repent, all ye ends of the earth, and come unto me and be baptized in my name, *that ye may be sanctified by the reception of the Holy Ghost,* that ye may stand spotless before me at the last day" (3 Nephi 27:20, emphasis added).

Elder Bruce R. McConkie wrote that to be sanctified is "to become clean, pure, and spotless; to be free from the blood and sins of the world."[12] Before we can be resurrected to inherit any degree of celestial glory, then, we must be sanctified before the Lord. To be sanctified is to be forgiven. However it is not an "absolute guarantee" of being saved (see D&C 20: 32–34).[13]

When we truly receive the Holy Ghost—which is a significantly different experience than receiving a mere prompting from the still small voice—we may know that we are forgiven. Although the power of the Holy Ghost can be felt by many who may or may not have yet entered into the covenant of the Atonement through baptism, the direct receipt of the Holy Ghost is a much more rare, although readily available, sacred occurrence. Because the Holy Ghost cannot dwell in an unclean tabernacle, "it is through his power as a Spirit Being that men may be sanctified and washed clean from all sin."[14] Forgiveness is therefore either inherently prerequisite to, or simultaneous with, the direct ministration of the Holy Ghost.

---

12. McConkie, *Mormon Doctrine*, 675.

13. Ibid., 676.

14. Ibid., 677.

CHAPTER FIVE
The Repentance Process

> And now, it came to pass that when King Benjamin had thus spoken to his people, he sent among them, desiring to know of his people if they believed the words which he had spoken unto them. And they all cried with one voice, saying: Yea, we believe all the words which thou hast spoken unto us; and also, we know of their surety and truth, because of the Spirit of the Lord Omnipotent, which has wrought a mighty change in us, or in our hearts, that we have no more disposition to do evil, but to do good continually.
>
> —*Mosiah 5:1–2*

KING BENJAMIN TAUGHT HIS PEOPLE POWERFUL DOCTRINE. The Spirit of the Lord testified to the truth of his words, and they believed. The consequences of their faith in and their obedience to King Benjamin's teachings was that the same "mighty change" experienced by Alma was also felt by this multitude at that time.

It is noteworthy that the people of King Benjamin described their transformation as having received a complete overhaul of their desires, and that they had "no more disposition to do evil, but to do good continually." Sin was not enticing or attractive to them any longer; they sought only to do the works of righteousness. These scripture verses contain an important but significantly encapsulated account of the repentance process of an entire people. But what the brevity of this account does not reveal is the marvelous but excruciating personal stories of each individual penitent soul who shared this experience and their efforts to overcome sin and transgression to obtain forgiveness. They could not have received this dramatic degree of changed heart without having also willingly and faithfully walked the complete pathway of repentance.

Having entered the waters of baptism, Latter-day Saints should realize the significance of the Atonement of Jesus Christ as the center point of Heavenly Father's plan for His children. We are not unlike the people of King Benjamin in this regard. Although we cannot completely comprehend it, we should also have an appreciation for the precise completeness of the Savior's sacrifice on our behalf.

Exactitude and unity is required to enter into the covenant. It had been required of Jesus, and it is required of us as well. As we understand this important principle, we begin to realize that the Lord requires exactness and completeness in our efforts to repent.

Repentance is exacting. Indeed, it must be. It can be a powerful temptation to bypass or gloss over one or more of the requirements to repentance, particularly those that are the most uncomfortable, inconvenient, or painful for us. However, just as it was required of the Savior to "suffer both body and spirit"(D&C 19:18) in completeness in order to bring about the Atonement, so must we repent in fulness—in body and spirit—to qualify for its blessings.

STEP 1: RECOGNIZING SIN

There has never been a time in which Satan has been more successful in camouflaging sin than today. Our culture celebrates freedom of choice above all else. Where freedom to choose is so protected, venerated, and honored, it can be difficult for some to understand that some choices are inherently evil. When our academia adopts and promotes the intellectual philosophy that truth is relative to our circumstances, the very standards of right and wrong become deeply hidden and our society suffers the consequences.

Frequently, sin has been disguised from many by the simple act of re-packaging and re-branding the activities that were previously generally recognized as wrong. Reborn as "alternative lifestyles," sin has increasingly been made more socially acceptable at every level. Elder David B. Haight has said:

> One of Satan's methods is to distract and entice us so that we will take our eyes off the dangerous crevasses. He has succeeded to such an extent that many no longer recognize sin as sin. Movies, television, and magazines have glorified sin into what they think is an acceptable lifestyle and there is no punishment for evil behavior. Assuredly we live in a time spoken of by Isaiah when men "call evil

good, and good evil" (Isaiah 5:20). Don't trifle with evil. You will lose. Don't display the somewhat arrogant attitude of those who say, "I can handle it," or "Everyone else does it."[1]

Recognizing sin is a great challenge. As Elder Haight taught, Satan has been extremely successful at lowering society's standards for morality, ethics and virtue, while at the same time raising our tolerance and appetite for both evil and the "appearance of evil."

Our spiritual senses and sensibilities are numbed by constant exposure to sin that is camouflaged as desirable pleasures of the world. Along with movies, television, and magazines, we can add the power of degrading music, the popularity of shock radio, and the explosion of internet pornography to the list of influences that we far too often invite into our homes. Exposure to some of these influences is sin of itself.

Even less obvious influences can have an impact on our ability to recognize sin. For example, when the popular media and culture teaches us that biting sarcasm is an acceptable form of humor or communication in our relationships, we are likely to be less able to recognize when our fashionably snappy responses have offended others, including the Spirit. Sin, or potential sin, can be dressed in the trappings of humor, music, art, competition, wealth, or any number of other forms that are generally acceptable to the world. We are surrounded by constant examples of evil being called good and good things becoming evil, as Isaiah prophesied.

If Satan can, through his deception, deaden us as to the existence of our sins, it makes it impossible for us to repent. When we do not recognize our sins, neither do we acknowledge why our sins are wrong in the first place. In that state, we cannot understand the implications of our actions and will not recognize that someone has even been wronged or damaged, even if that someone is us.

Another potential challenge to the process of recognizing sin is in understanding the definition of sin itself. What is sin? "All unrighteousness is sin: and there is a sin not unto death" (1 John 5:17). "Whosoever committeth sin transgresseth also the law: for sin is the transgression of the law" (1 John 3:4).

In its pure form, sin is an overt act which the sinner knowingly

---

1. David B. Haight, *A Light Unto the World*, (Salt Lake City: Deseret Book, 1997) 142–143.

commits in opposition to the commandments of God or the Light of Christ. Sin is an open rebellion to the will of God. Murder is the darkest example of that type of rebellion; however there are a great many sins that fall into this category. These obvious sins are usually the easiest to recognize.

Another type of sin exists when we fail to do something we should have done. These sins may not be so obvious. The sinner does not knowingly commit a sin but instead may knowingly fail to act when he should. As James wrote: "Therefore to him that knoweth to do good, and doeth it not, to him it is sin" (James 4:17).

Many have a tendency to think of sins of omission as if they are the "minor sins" in comparison to the "major sins" against the commandments. This is a dangerous view, for we do not know that God grades sin with a palette of increasingly gradient grays. All sin—or any sin, no matter the perceived degree—will make us unclean and unworthy to return to the presence of God. To that end, sins of omission ultimately have the same spiritual result as if we had overtly broken a commandment.

When we, as members of Christ's Church, fail to develop and demonstrate our faith in the Savior, when we live our lives without hope of the Redemption, when we do not show forth the pure love of Christ toward our fellowman, we sin by our omissions. To refuse to serve where called, to fail to keep covenants of consecration, to not sustain our Church leaders, to fail to act on spiritual promptings, to fail to study the scriptures, or to pray in a meaningful way all constitute sins of omission. These omissions are frequently sins against our own personal inspiration in which we demonstrate our unworthiness of and our unpreparedness for the gift of the Holy Ghost.

Consider the example of the Savior. Even after having lived a perfect life, what would the impact have been had He omitted the Atonement? The Father's plan for the redemption of His children would have failed! To the extent that we can also become saviors on mount Zion (see Obadiah 1:21), we also have a serious obligation not to omit the things that ultimately assist in bringing others, including our kindred dead, unto Christ. To omit these important elements of the gospel of Jesus Christ is to sin before the Lord.

Jesus condemned the scribes and Pharisees over their omissions, demonstrating the seriousness of these sins in the Savior's eyes: "Woe unto you, scribes and Pharisees, hypocrites! for ye pay tithe of mint and anise and cumin, and have omitted the weightier matters of the law, judgment, mercy and faith: these ought ye to have done, and not to leave the other undone. Ye blind guides, which strain at a gnat, and swallow a camel" (Matthew 23:23–24).

President Harold B. Lee taught that another sin of omission includes failure to forgive, for "one may sin by being hasty in judgment on vital issues or where the welfare of a human soul is at stake."[2] The Doctrine and Covenants teaches that "He that forgiveth not his brother his trespasses standeth condemned before the Lord; for there remaineth in him the greater sin" (D&C 64:9).

There is also a broad spectrum of experiences in life that may or may not constitute formal sin. For my purposes, I would label the more severe of these experiences "transgressions," when they are not knowingly committed but when the laws of heaven are nevertheless transgressed. Transgression also requires repentance when we are made aware of the error.

In much of the literature of the Church, the terms "sin" and "transgression" are used interchangeably. There is validity in this transposable usage because they both involve the violation—or transgression—of a law. But it is significant that we refer to Adam's partaking of the fruit of the tree of knowledge of good and evil—in direct disobedience to God's expressed command—as "Adam's transgression" (second article of faith) and not as "original sin," a term used by much of the rest of Christianity. Adam and Eve had no capacity for knowledge of good and evil until they partook of the fruit of the tree. Notwithstanding, their action—their transgression—had unavoidable consequences, and repentance would forever be a part of their lives and the lives of their children. Sin requires knowledge of the law. A transgression can occur through ignorance, although the law is nevertheless broken.

I recall meeting with a sister who was a new convert to the Church. She had only been baptized for three or four months when she asked to see me as her bishop. There had been a lesson taught in Relief Society about tithes and offerings that brought her to the realization that she had, unknowingly, not been following the commandments properly. This was all pretty new to her, and although her desires were to be

---

2. *Teachings of Harold B. Lee, Eleventh President of The Church of Jesus Christ of Latter-day Saints*, ed. by Clyde J. Williams, (Salt Lake City: Bookcraft, 1996) 108.

fully obedient, she could only be obedient to principles that she understood. While the fact was that her tithing had not been fully paid—she was in transgression of the law—she had not understood the principle of tithing properly. She had not sinned against what she knew; she had transgressed unknowingly. And, when she became aware of the error, she made the necessary corrections and repented.

This illustrates why it is so incumbent upon us to gain knowledge "by study and also by faith" (D&C 88:118) pertaining to the gospel of Jesus Christ and the commandments of God. In ignorance of the law, we are all transgressors. We cannot repent without the knowledge that is necessary for us to recognize our sins. "Knowledge saves a man; and in the world of spirits no man can be exalted but by knowledge. So long as a man will not give heed to the commandments, he must abide without salvation. If a man has knowledge, he can be saved."[3] "It is impossible for a man to be saved in ignorance" (D&C 131:6).

Whatever form or perceived degree of sin we may experience, we must have the knowledge, intelligence, and ability to recognize our mistakes in order to overcome them and gain forgiveness. Further, on this principle, Moroni recorded the following words of the Lord that teach us that recognizing our sins is a critical part of the "line-upon-line" process that turns our weaknesses into strengths: "And if men come unto me I will show unto them their weakness. I give unto men weakness that they may be humble; and my grace is sufficient for all men that humble themselves before me; for if they humble themselves before me, and have faith in me, then will I make weak things become strong unto them" (Ether 12:27).

Having a basic understanding of gospel principles will certainly help us in this process. Scripture study will teach and remind us of God's commandments. Heeding the counsel of our Prophet, Apostles and other Church leaders will also teach us to recognize sin. President Kimball wrote:

> When we come to recognize our sin sincerely and without reservations, we are ready to follow such processes as will rid us of sin's effects. Enos sets us a good example. As he began to realize his true

---

3. Joseph Smith Jr., *History of the Church of Jesus Christ of Latter-day Saints*, ed. by B. H. Roberts, (Salt Lake City: Deseret News Press, 1902–12) 6:314.

status before his Maker, he pondered upon his condition how he had been born in the faith and trained by a good father who had taught him righteousness and the nurture and admonitions of the Lord. When he found himself far out of hearing, deep in the forest where he was alone with himself, he began to convict himself of his sins. Eternal life began to loom up as something much to be desired, and he says: "the words [of] . . . eternal life, and the joy of the saints, sunk deep into my heart, and my soul hungered."

Now that he had convinced himself that he was in desperate straits, he began to put his mind in order. "I kneeled down before my Maker," he said, "and I cried unto him in mighty prayer and supplication for mine own soul."

The sincerity of his change of heart is manifested in his extended efforts to make his adjustment and get forgiveness: "And all the day long did I cry unto him; yea, and when the night came I did still raise my voice high that it reached the heavens" (Enos 1:4).

When this spirit is in the transgressor and he has placed himself at the mercy of the Lord, he begins to receive the relief which will eventually develop into total repentance.[4]

For a member of the Church who has received the gift of the Holy Ghost, another barometer for recognizing sin in our lives is in the presence or absence of the Spirit. The Holy Ghost flees when sin is present in our lives. Its ministration is subject to our obedience to the commandments. When the Holy Ghost is not part of our lives, we have either done something to alienate us from our Father in Heaven, or we have failed to do something which would have kept the Spirit with us. In either case, recognizing our sin and repenting is the proper prescription for our spiritual health.

STEP 2: REMORSE

"Now I rejoice, not that ye were made sorry, but that ye sorrowed to repentance; for ye were made sorry after a godly manner, that ye might receive damage by us in nothing; For godly sorrow worketh repentance to salvation not to be repented of; but the sorrow of the world worketh death" (JST 2 Corinthians 7:9–10). I have had the opportunity to sit in counsel many times with members who came to

---

4. Spencer W. Kimball, *The Miracle of Forgiveness,* (Salt Lake City: Bookcraft, 1971) 157.

me for assistance in their process of repentance. I have met with individuals who openly acknowledged sin but were not very sorry about it. They had myriad reasons or excuses that they felt explained away their behavior. Others I have counseled with were indeed sorry that their sins were discovered, and even expressed a consequential interest in changing their behavior, but they had no righteous desire to repent, for they had frankly enjoyed their sins. They almost savored them.

I can tell you that those counseling sessions were virtually devoid of the Spirit. These individuals had not "cried unto Him in mighty prayer and supplication for [their] own soul[s]" as Enos described. The Spirit was not in them because they were not truly repentant. "For godly sorrow worketh repentance," wrote Paul. Perhaps Paul meant that only godly sorrow worketh repentance.

Those experiences could have been—and should have been—the cause of great joy. Unfortunately, however, their experience was as the prophet Mormon wrote: "Their sorrowing was not unto repentance, because of the goodness of God; but it was rather the sorrowing of the damned, because the Lord would not always suffer them to take happiness in sin" (Mormon 2:13).

I have also had the precious and sacred opportunity to counsel with members who came to me as their bishop in the depths of humility, having what I can only describe properly as "godly sorrow" for their actions. The Spirit was strong. They had fasted. They had immersed themselves in the scriptures. They had spent considerable time on their knees in the preceding days, weeks, and months. Their sorrow had truly worked repentance to their salvation.

Occasionally these circumstances surrounded repentance of sins that were of a very serious nature; sometimes they were not. Nevertheless, I have learned that the element of godly sorrow is consistent with the truly penitent, no matter the size of the sin.

> The truly repentant man is sorry before he is apprehended. He is sorry even if his secret is never known. He desires to make voluntary amends. The culprit has not "godly sorrow" who must be found out by being reported or by chains of circumstances which finally bring the offense to light. The thief is not repentant who continues in grave offenses until he is caught. Repentance of the godly type means that one comes to recognize the sin and voluntarily and without

pressure from outside sources begins his transformation.[5]

Godly sorrow also leads the sinner to such a repentant and humble state of being that he or she is willing to accept any consequence that will result in obtaining forgiveness. The man with true godly sorrow is not concerned about "how it will look" if he is subject to formal Church discipline, even if it includes excommunication, for he understands that any such consequence is designed to assist him in his repentance, and is a necessary step. He will not fear man more than God, and he knows that by accepting whatever perceived punishment is meted out, he can do what is in his power to show his Heavenly Father that he is sincere in his desire to obtain forgiveness.

Perhaps this attitude is what is meant when the scriptures refer to a broken heart and contrite spirit, and why it is the required sacrifice for sinners. "The righteous cry, and the Lord heareth, and delivereth them out of all their troubles. The Lord is nigh unto them that are of a broken heart; and saveth such as be of a contrite spirit" (Psalm 34:17–18). The Psalms go on to teach, "For thou desirest not sacrifice; else would I give it: thou delightest not in burnt offering. The sacrifices of God are a broken spirit: a broken and a contrite heart, O God, thou wilt not despise" (Psalm 51:16–17).

> And men are instructed sufficiently that they know good from evil. And the law is given unto men. And by the law no flesh is justified; or, by the law men are cut off. Yea, by the temporal law they were cut off; and also, by the spiritual law they perish from that which is good, and become miserable forever.
>
> Wherefore, redemption cometh in and through the Holy Messiah; for he is full of grace and truth.
>
> Behold, he offereth himself a sacrifice for sin, to answer the ends of the law, unto all those who have a broken heart and a contrite spirit; and unto none else can the ends of the law be answered. (2 Nephi 2:5–7)

One cannot achieve a state of godly sorrow, complete with a broken heart and contrite spirit without being thoroughly humbled before the Lord. In fact, the word *contrite* is derived from a Latin past participle meaning to bruise, to grind, and to crush. A contrite heart, then, is an essential characteristic of the penitent soul, which brings us very much at-one with the Savior, who suffered for our sins in Gethsemane,

---

5. Kimball, *The Miracle of Forgiveness*, 153–154.

or the place of the olive press. There, Jesus, like the olives in the press under the immense grinding stone, was subject to the infinite crushing weight of the sins of the world. Mark tells us in his gospel that Christ was "sore amazed" at the intensity of this experience (Mark 14:33). Luke describes the way the Savior bore his burden as "being in agony" (Luke 22:44). Contrition, then, follows the example of the Savior. In fact, one could say that contrition is Christ-like.

STEP 3: CONFESSING SIN

Confession is an essential element of true repentance. It is, in many ways, a natural by-product of the process. Confession of sin is one of the sweetest tasting fruit that repentance bears. It cleanses not only the conscience but also the spirit of the sinner to openly confess wrongdoing to the Lord to those whom we have offended and, in some instances, to the Lord's representative, a common judge in Israel. "Behold, he who has repented of his sins, the same is forgiven, and I, the Lord, remember them no more. By this ye may know if a man repenteth of his sins—behold, he will confess them and forsake them" (D&C 58:42–43).

I have seen the dramatic physical change that occurs in an individual in the time it takes to make full, proper confession. Those who seek counsel with their bishop in this process carry themselves differently walking out of the bishop's office than they did when they walked in. Yet, even that dramatic change is merely symbolic of the more dramatic changes that occur within.

The long-term impact of dealing with stress and guilt associated with carrying the burden of sin is immense. It takes a terrible toll in not only the spiritual life but also the physical health of the individual. Speaking of the impact of sinners partaking of the sacrament unworthily, Paul taught: "But let a man examine himself, and so let him eat of that bread, and drink of that cup. For he that eateth and drinketh unworthily, eateth and drinketh damnation to himself, not discerning the Lord's body. For this cause many are weak and sickly among you, and many sleep" (1 Corinthians 11:28–30).

Paul certainly suggests a connection between health and sin. While the experience of Job teaches us clearly that the relationship between sin and sickness is not necessarily cause-and-effect, science has only begun to understand the impact that stress has on our physical health. Who can question but that sin causes extreme stress that effects us physically in many negative ways? Perhaps many are "weak and sickly" among us even now as the result of the physical effects of unrepentant, unconfessed sin.

Many have expressed feeling the weight of the world lifted from them as they have gone in humility to the Lord's designated servant and representative to confess sin. This common experience is intentionally and divinely designed, for the Lord Jesus Christ has given us the promise: "Come unto me, all ye that labour and are heavy laden, and I will give you rest. Take my yoke upon you, and learn of me; for I am meek and lowly in heart: and ye shall find rest unto your souls. For my yoke is easy, and my burden is light" (Matthew 11:28–30).

Throughout his life, President Kimball taught extensively about the need for confession in order to make repentance complete. Many Church members wonder what guidelines exist for determining the need to confess to a bishop. On this matter, President Kimball wrote:

> Especially grave errors such as sexual sins shall be confessed to the bishop as well as to the Lord. There are two remissions that one might wish to have: first, the forgiveness from the Lord, and second, the forgiveness of the Lord's Church through its leaders. As soon as one has an inner conviction of his sins, he should go to the Lord in "mighty prayer," as did Enos, and never cease his supplications until he shall, like Enos, receive the assurance that his sins have been forgiven by the Lord. It is unthinkable that God absolves serious sins upon a few requests. He is likely to wait until there has been long-sustained repentance as evidenced by a willingness to comply with all his other requirements. So far as the Church is concerned, no priest nor elder is authorized by virtue of that calling to perform this act for the Church. The Lord has a consistent, orderly plan. Every soul in the organized stakes is given a bishop who, by the very nature of his calling and his ordination, is a "judge in Israel." In the missions, a branch president fills that responsibility. The bishop may be one's best earthly friend. He will hear the problems, judge the seriousness thereof, determine the degree of adjustment, and decide if it warrants an eventual forgiveness. He does this as the earthly representative of God, who is the master physician, the master psychologist, the master psychiatrist. If repentance is sufficient, he may waive penalties, which is tantamount to forgiveness so far as the Church's organization is concerned. The bishop claims no authority to absolve sins, but he does share the burden, waive penalties, relieve

tension and strain, and he may assure a continuation of Church activity. He will keep the whole matter most confidential.[6]

> Clearly, all sexual sin must be confessed to a bishop as a common judge. Abuse of the god-like powers of creation of life are especially grievous to our Heavenly Father, and has especially grievous eternal consequences. Such sins cannot be casually repented of. I am not going to attempt to delineate every specific sexual sin. There is a certain danger in that. However, the scriptures teach, and the Spirit testifies, that sexual sin involves far more than just inappropriate intercourse. It also includes "anything like unto it." (D&C 59:6)

Even so, a matter need not be as weighty as that in order to justify counseling with a bishop. Any sin, transgression, or misdeed that separates us from our Heavenly Father and the influence of His Spirit, where our direct petitions to our Father still leave us feeling spiritually uncertain or where we continue to struggle under the weight of temptation, is worthy of a bishop's counsel and guidance.

The bishop's role and purpose in this is not, after all, to condemn the sinner. Instead, in a spirit of love and reconciliation, he is there to gently guide the member through a process of repentance that, no doubt, he has himself also gone through to one degree or another.

From a bishop's perspective, there exists an abiding sense of compassion and understanding that creates a special bond with the member. Aside from my own family, there are few people on earth that I have greater love and respect for than those I have counseled with through the process of repentance and seen take upon them the image and countenance that Alma describes (see Alma 5:14).

STEP 4: RESTITUTION

> If a thief be found breaking up, and be smitten that he die, there shall no blood be shed for him.
>
> If the sun be risen upon him, there shall be blood shed for him; for he should make full restitution; if he have nothing, then he shall be sold for his theft.
>
> If the theft be certainly found in his hand alive, whether it be ox, or ass, or sheep; he shall restore double.
>
> If a man shall cause a field or vineyard to be eaten, and shall put

---

6. Spencer W. Kimball, *Faith Precedes the Miracle,* 181.

in his beast, and shall feed in another man's field; of the best of his own field, and of the best of his own vineyard, shall he make restitution.

If fire break out, and catch in thorns, so that the stacks of corn, or the standing corn, or the field, be consumed therewith; he that kindled the fire shall surely make restitution. (Exodus 22:2–6)

Restitution for sin is a central, straightforward, and essential requirement of every sinner who hopes to obtain forgiveness. To make full restitution is to completely restore that which was lost due to the consequence of sin and will usually require some degree of sacrifice. The level of sacrifice involved is often directly related to the seriousness of the sin.

If restitution is too easy in relation to the gravity of the sin, then true humility may not be part of the process. For the course of repentance to accomplish the "mighty change" described by Alma, the depths of humility must eventually be reached. The requirement for restitution assures that the sinner has ample opportunity to humble himself appropriately. Those who try to avoid this experience, whether out of embarrassment, lack of commitment, or pride, can never experience the cleansing fulness of forgiveness.

How can we possibly hope to have access to Christ's unlimited atoning powers if we withhold our total willingness to do what is required of us? As Elder Bruce R. McConkie wrote:

> Every repentant person desires by instinct to make amends for the wrongs he has done. The desire to make reparation is an outgrowth of godly sorrow. Has property or money been taken—it must be returned. Has character been defamed or the truth maligned—now the truth must be spoken. Saul the persecutor must become Paul the defender. Restitution is not always possible, but it must always be made insofar as it can be; the repentant sinner must give whatever equivalent he can to compensate for the loss he has caused. When he has done all he can, the Lord will accept his offering.[7]

For some sins, determining proper restitution is fairly straightforward. Where a monetary loss exists, the money can be replaced exactly or with interest. If an object of specific value is damaged, it can generally be fixed or replaced. In simple terms, the child who takes

---

7. Bruce R. McConkie, *A New Witness for the Articles of Faith*, (Salt Lake City: Deseret Book, 1985) 237.

candy from a store can be brought back to the scene of the crime to apologize and pay for the treat.

However, in many cases it can be impossible to accurately put a price on that which is lost to sin. For example, what value can be placed on a loss of faith, hope, charity, or virtue? How can one replace broken trust or heal a broken heart? How do you fix damaged integrity or repair an injured self-image? When we cause this kind of harm—as we inevitably do—making true, full, and complete restitution may be impossible for us, no matter what we try to do.

I have often wondered if this is the reason the scriptures teach the connection between forgiveness and our efforts to bring souls unto Christ. While we may not have power to restore or replace these priceless treasures when they are lost as a result of our actions, perhaps we do have the capacity to build and strengthen these same elements in the lives of others. This principle is taught repeatedly throughout the scriptures.

"For behold the field is white already to harvest; and lo, he that thrusteth in his sickle with his might, the same layeth up in store that he perisheth not, but bringeth salvation to his soul" (D&C 4:4). In this revelation on missionary work, the Lord promises that by the efforts of those that "embark in the service of God" salvation is brought to the soul of the missionary. Perhaps this is the principle of restitution as it applies to that loss which cannot be replaced. Other scriptures teach this as well:

> Therefore, thrust in your sick with all your soul, and your sins are forgiven you, and you shall be laden with sheaves upon your back. (D&C 31:5)

> For I will forgive you of your sins with this commandment—that you remain steadfast in your minds in solemnity and the spirit of prayer, in bearing testimony to all the world of those things which are communicated unto you. (D&C 84:61)

> Brethren, if any of you do err from the truth, and one convert him;
> Let him know that he which converteth the sinner from the error of his way shall save a soul from death, and shall hide a multitude of sins. (James 5:19–20)

The lives of Alma the Younger and the sons of Mosiah are wonderful examples of this principle in action. They were part of a "rising generation that could not understand the words" of their prophet, King Benjamin (Mosiah 27:1).

> Now the sons of Mosiah were numbered among the unbelievers; and also one of the sons of Alma was numbered among them, he being called Alma, after his father; nevertheless, he became a very wicked and an idolatrous man. And he was a man of many words, and did speak much flattery to the people; therefore he led many of the people to do after the manner of his iniquities.
>
> And he became a great hindrance to the prosperity of the Church of God; stealing away the hearts of the people; giving a chance for the enemy of God to exercise his power over them. (Mosiah 27:8–9)

They spent a considerable amount of time and effort "seeking to destroy the Church of God" (Alma 36:6). They did so in secrecy, in direct rebellion to the King and the commandments of God (see Mosiah 27:10–11). Who can calculate the tremendous damage to spiritual intangibles of faith, hope, and charity that these men caused in the hearts and minds of the people? Think of the broken hearts of their parents, who had dedicated themselves to building the Church. What kind of damage did they do to their reputations and to the reputations of their families and to ministries of their fathers? They were more than a mere "hindrance" to the Church; they were a cancer. Was it possible for them to make a full and complete restitution for the many lost testimonies and shattered lives for which they were responsible? Not directly.

However, the scriptures indicate that after their conversion, Alma and the sons of Mosiah "from that time forth . . . labored without ceasing, that [they] might bring souls unto repentance; that [they] might bring them to taste of the exceeding joy" that Alma and his brethren had experienced (Alma 36:24). Over time, as they taught the gospel and brought souls unto Christ, it was given to Alma and his brethren to establish faith, increase hope and build charity in the lives of many others. Ultimately, the requirement of offering restitution, as a necessary step in their personal repentance, was fulfilled.

Throughout our life, we are frequently hurt in this same manner. Since we recognize that we can experience loss in ways that cannot be replaced, we may be tempted to believe that those who have wronged us are not deserving of forgiveness. We may be tempted to harbor resentment and bitterness as a result. In times such as those, we must have the courage and the faith to cast our burden on the Lord and simply refuse to carry it any longer. "Come unto me, all ye that labour and are heavy laden, and I will give you rest. Take my yoke upon you, and learn of me; for I am meek and lowly in heart: and ye shall find rest unto your souls. For my yoke is easy, and my burden is light" (Matthew 11:28–30).

The Restoration of the gospel in the last days, through the prophet Joseph, is spoken of as the "restitution of all things" prophesied by Peter (Acts 3:21). I have contemplated on many levels the promise that has been given that the Savior will bring about this universal restitution. There is great meaning here.

The telestial world in which we find ourselves, filled as it is with misery, suffering, and abuse, is the consequence of sin and transgression on the earth. This is the reason the earth must needs "be renewed and receive its paradisiacal glory" (tenth article of faith). To some extent, each of us is an innocent wayfarer in this setting, challenged with the trial of enduring through the despair we experience in our own life and witness in the lives of others. Who cannot tell of immense personal loss at the hands of others? To another extent, we are each active participants in continuing this worldly environment as we take turns passing around the pain and by hurting others through our words, thoughts, and deeds.

The promise of the Savior, however, is that none of this damage needs to be permanent. Whether the costs of sin are taking their toll in our life, our home, our community, or our world (which they certainly are), through Christ's Atonement we are promised that all of these tragedies are only temporary. "I say unto thee, my son, that the plan of restoration is requisite with the justice of God; for it is requisite that all things should be restored to their proper order" (Alma 41:2).

Through repentance and the Atonement, there will be a restitution of all things. Wherever there has been loss, there will be a restoration. Wherever there exists lasting scars, whether physical or emotional, there will be healing. As we labor individually to make restitution in relatively small matters, the Lord fulfills the promised restoration on a much grander scale. This doctrine is discussed more completely in chapter nine.

STEP 5: FORSAKE SIN

"By this ye may know if a man repenteth of his sins—behold he will confess and forsake them" (D&C 58:43). To forsake sin means to completely renounce, abandon and turn away from them. Once we have thus forsaken our sin, we cannot return to our former ways. To do so is to bring all the consequences of our former sins back upon our heads. Brigham Young also taught this principle in a discourse to the priesthood of the Church:

> Suppose we admit of malice, anger, and wrath in our hearts,— steep ourselves in wickedness, by taking the name of God in vain, by entering into every kind of outbreak and transgression, by defiance to every wholesome law, by neglecting our families, physically, mentally and morally, and by neglecting our brethren and ourselves, our former repentance and baptism for the remission of sins will not profit us, through indulging in sin afterwards; but all our former sins will again be upon us, and we must atone for the whole. Then let us cleave unto righteousness, learn to do well, and continue to do so all the days of our lives, that our former sins may not stand against us. This is our duty.[8]

The Doctrine and Covenants adds: "And now, verily I say unto you I, the Lord, will not lay any sin to your charge; go your ways and sin no more; but unto that soul who sinneth shall the former sins return, saith the Lord your God" (D&C 82:7).

One of the impacts of true repentance includes a desire to abandon sin not only permanently but also completely. This desire comes from the impact of true godly sorrow on the sinner's soul. Because real, effectual repentance brings one to a closer, more intimate, and more complete understanding of the Savior's sacrifice, a desire to turn away from sin is a natural and divinely appointed consequence of the repentance experience.

It is interesting to note that the scripture refers to forsaking "sins" instead of "sin." I think there is a very important lesson here. It has been my experience—in my own life and in counseling with others— that the need for repentance is often called to our attention by a singular sin. Frequently, however, that particular sin is connected to others in a chain of events. I have never found that a sin generally regarded as serious, such as adultery, was ever entered into in a vacuum. Other

8. *Journal of Discourses*, 6:316

sins nearly always precede it and follow it. Precursor sins commonly include violations of the Word of Wisdom, bearing false witness, coveting, lusting in one's heart, failure to attend meetings, not sustaining Church leaders, and so forth. At one level, then, repentance invariably involves overcoming more than one sin at a time: both the primary sin that started the process in the first place and all those other sins connected to it in either leading to or covering up our more serious sins.

However, I believe there is another, more compelling reason that the scripture refers to forsaking sin in the plural. Consider that everything about repentance points us directly to the Atonement—the very process by which we can become one with our Father and His Son. When an individual truly accesses the covenant of the Atonement and Christ's infinite sacrifice through repentance, it is not and cannot be in a limited way. How can someone humble themselves, feel godly sorrow, suffer a broken heart and a contrite spirit, and be willing to make any restitution and confession necessary to obtain forgiveness without feeling so about all sin? Can an infinite sacrifice be accessed in such a finite manner?

True repentance leads the sin-bound soul to desire to sin no more in any degree. When we become one with God, then like Him, we "cannot look upon sin with the least degree of allowance" (D&C 1:31), either. Therefore, the Lord sets the standard in the fifty-eighth section of the Doctrine and Covenants for identifying one who has truly repented: "Behold, he will confess and forsake them" (D&C 58:43). In other words, he will confess and forsake them all—not just one or two sins. He desires to bring his soul into full compliance with the commandments of God, not just partial compliance.

The connection here is an important one: We cannot bring only our most dominant, our favorite, our easiest to overcome, our most hidden, our deepest and darkest, or our most obvious sin to the altar of repentance without bringing them all. To forsake a specific sin in the context of true repentance, we must forsake them all. Yet the promise and blessing for doing so is clear—and clearly worth it: "Verily, thus saith the Lord: It shall come to pass that every soul who forsaketh his sins and cometh unto me, and calleth on my name, and obeyeth my commandments, shall see my face and know that I am" (D&C 93:1).

CHAPTER SIX

Satan's Alternatives to Repentance

And, behold, Satan hath put it into their hearts to alter the words which you have caused to be written, or which you have translated, which have gone out of your hands. And behold, I say unto you, that because they have altered the words, they read contrary from that which was translated and caused to be written; And on this wise, the devil has sought to lay a cunning plan, that he may destroy this work.

—*Doctrine and Covenants 10:10–12*

THE PLAN OF HAPPINESS WAS PRESENTED TO ALL of our Heavenly Father's children before the world was created. In that setting we were taught the principles of obedience, agency, repentance, and the need for faith in Jesus Christ, who would come to earth as our Savior, to redeem us from our sins by His atoning sacrifice. The new and everlasting covenant was explained to us clearly, and we understood then—certainly better than we do now—the role that obedience to the laws and ordinances of the gospel of Jesus Christ would have in our opportunity to return to God's presence, graced with increased knowledge, wisdom, and power. We understood our eternal capacity, if we used our agency wisely, to become like our heavenly parents.

The scriptures record the joy with which this instruction was received by those who kept their first estate and chose to follow, accept, and sustain Jesus as our Savior and Redeemer: "Where wast thou when I laid the foundations of the earth? Declare, if thou hast understanding. Who hath laid the measures thereof, if thou knowest? Or who hath stretched the line upon it? Whereupon are the foundations thereof fastened? Or who laid the corner stone thereof; when the morning stars sang together, and all the sons of God shouted for joy?"(Job 38: 4–7).

Yet, a full third of the hosts of heaven chose not to keep their first estate. Instead they were swayed by the arguments proposed by Lucifer, an impressive leader in his own right. What if Jesus could not live the perfect life that would be required of Him? What if He succumbed to the trials and temptations that would snare the rest of us? Where would that leave us—forever lost without any hope at all? God's entire plan rested on the ability of the Firstborn to fulfill His foreordained role. And yet, we also understood that Jesus would experience the same "veil of forgetfulness" that would test the rest of us. He would have to increase "in wisdom and stature and in favour with God" (Luke 2:52) until He would come to understand fully not only who He was but also what He needed to do on earth to salvage Heavenly Father's children in the eternities.

THE ANTI-CHRIST APPROACH

What if Jesus failed? Lucifer's arguments were persuasive. For one of every three of "all the sons of God," God's plan simply contained too much risk. Lucifer put forth his alternative plan, saying: "Behold, here am I, send me, I will be thy son, and I will redeem all mankind, that one soul shall not be lost, and surely I will do it; wherefore give me thine honor" (Moses 4:1).

This was a compelling message to many: all reward and no risk. Even if we set aside the discussion that Lucifer's entire argument and platform was built on a lie—it could not produce the results that were attainable in God's plan—it was unfeasible because, in Lucifer's plan, God would cease to be God. The glory and honor of the Father would have to be transferred to Lucifer. There would be no need for a Redeemer; there would be no Atonement; there would be no saving ordinances or empowering covenants. In fact, in Lucifer's false substitute for the plan of redemption, no one other than Lucifer would have access to "all that the Father hath."

In Book of Mormon times, Korihor, an anti-Christ and a disciple of Satan, argued against the need for an atonement in a manner that likely reflects closely the arguments made by Satan himself in that premortal battle. It is easy to picture in the mind's eye, Satan confronting God and playing to his supporters using these words:

O ye that are bound down under a foolish and a vain hope, why do ye yoke yourselves with such foolish things? Why do ye look for a Christ? . . .

How do ye know of their surety? Behold, ye cannot know of things which ye do not see; therefore, ye cannot know that there shall be a Christ.

Ye look forward and say that ye see a remission of your sins. But behold, it is the effect of a frenzied mind. . . .

And many more such things did he say unto them, telling them that there could be no atonement made for the sins of men, but every man fared in this life according to the management of his creature; therefore every man prospered according to his genius, and that every man conquered according to his strength; and whatsoever a man did was no crime.

And thus he did preach unto them, leading away the hearts of many. (Alma 30:13–18)

Two-thirds of God's children were able to develop and exercise sufficient faith in Jesus that they supported Him, and through Him, the Father. This was probably accomplished through the testimonies and preaching of the gospel by "many of the noble and great ones" (Abraham 3:22) in a great missionary effort that is known to us generally as the War in Heaven. Amidst all the tumult, Jesus was perfectly obedient to the Father's plan; he was willing, submissive, and humble: "But, behold, my Beloved Son, which was my Beloved and Chosen from the beginning, said unto me—Father, thy will be done, and the glory be thine forever" (Moses 4:2).

Because of his rebellion, pride, and greed, the scripture records that Lucifer became Satan. He was thus awarded the fitting title "father of all lies" and was cast out of God's presence, along with those who followed him. He then began his work of darkness and destruction among the children of men on the earth.

Wherefore, because that Satan rebelled against me, and sought to destroy the agency of man, which I, the Lord God, had given him, and also, that I should give unto him mine own power; by the power of mine Only Begotten, I caused that he should be cast down;

And he became Satan, yea, even the devil, the father of all lies, to deceive and to blind men, and to lead them captive at his will, even as many as would not hearken unto my voice. (Moses 4:3–4)

Satan was not always who he is now. He was once a respected leader in the community of the heavens; a son of the morning. He certainly had the capacity—had he chosen differently—to become as one of the many "great and noble" sons of God. Instead, he became Satan through his rebellion to God's will and plan for His children. Satan simply insisted that he had "a better way" than the eternal truths that God proposed for us.

Satan continues his darkness and deception today using largely the same strategies and arguments that failed him before. Wherever God's plan has fixed requirements or "strait gates," Satan will sell "a better way," an easier path, or compelling arguments that appeal to our weaknesses. He doesn't need to always directly oppose truth—although he does plenty of that. Satan is also very successful in shading truth just enough that truth's essence is lost.

We should not be surprised, then, that Satan has attacked such an essential and necessary principle as repentance in many ways. Nephi, having seen our day, tells us something about the attitude of some people toward sin and repentance: "Yea, and there shall be many which shall say: Eat, drink, and be merry, for tomorrow we die; and it shall be well with us" (2 Nephi 28:7).

Those with this attitude have been duped and deceived into a direct opposition of the truth. There are many who live their lives with the philosophy of "eat, drink, and be merry, for tomorrow we die." They truly believe that their sins don't matter, that "it shall be well with them." They don't worry about the Resurrection or the Judgment, since they don't believe in those things, anyway.

However, there are many who cannot be swayed directly into thinking that there is no such thing as sin or that repentance is not necessary. Instead, many who consider themselves believers have grown comfortable with the conviction that most sin is insignificant, and a merciful God will overlook their faults; therefore, repentance is simply not a priority in their lives. Nephi spoke of these also:

> And there shall also be many which shall say: Eat, drink, and be merry; nevertheless, fear God—he will justify in committing a little sin; yea, lie a little, take the advantage of one because of his words, dig a pit for thy neighbor; there is no harm in this; and do all these things, for tomorrow we die; and if it so be that we are guilty, God will beat us with a few stripes, and at last we shall be saved in the kingdom of God. (2 Nephi 28:8)

Both of these philosophies represent clear and obvious false doctrine. They are Satan's attempts at presenting "a better way" that is contrary to the eternal principles of truth. Sometimes even active, devout members of the Church fall prey to pursuing "a better way" of overcoming faults or of perfecting ourselves in a manner that diminishes the significance of the Savior's sacrifice. The false doctrine present in these circumstances can be difficult to identify at times, sometimes influencing even the elect. The real danger to this enticement is in the fact that it comes by way of deception instead of by temptation: "For there shall arise false Christs, and false prophets, and shall shew great signs and wonders; insomuch that, if it were possible, they shall deceive the very elect" (Matthew 24:24).

It is not as if the elect necessarily choose to abandon a life of righteousness and suddenly give way to temptations to flagrantly disobey the commandments (although that can happen). Instead, the scripture seems to clearly indicate that the elect, "if it were possible" for them to be overcome by Satan, become deceived. They accept and believe in a counterfeit Christ, fraudulent representatives, and a fake gospel. In other words, they replace Christ with some new idea, philosophy, technology, person, or program.

It is imperative that we are not deceived in this manner. In the forty-fifth section of the Doctrine and Covenants, the Lord makes a reference to the parable of the ten virgins that contains vivid implications that those who are deceived will bear terrible consequences: "For they that are wise and have received the truth, and have taken the Holy Spirit for their guide, and have not been deceived—verily I say unto you, they shall not be hewn down and cast into the fire, but shall abide the day" (D&C 45:57).

Perhaps one reason we are continually counseled to read, study, and ponder the scriptures, to fast and pray, and to follow the counsel of the living prophet is because by doing so we become intimately familiar with God's revealed standards. Knowledge of God's standards—and they aren't called the standard works for nothing—protects us from deception. When we take the steps necessary to become personally and thoroughly familiar with the true source of all salvation, when we know the voice of the true Shepherd who calls us, then we are less likely to be deceived by false Christs. However, if our attempts to come unto Christ are half-hearted and our desires are lukewarm, we may fail to recognize the voice of our Savior and are then more likely to be deceived by Satan when he floats his deceptions past us.

A friend of mine compared this concept with the experience of being a fresh, green missionary landing in a foreign country for the first time. The currency, he said, at first looked like "monopoly money." Because he wasn't familiar with the real currency, or because the real currency was foreign to him, anyone could have fooled him with any type of counterfeit currency. He wouldn't have known otherwise. It wasn't until he became familiar with the local culture, the setting, the language, and the currency that it would be more difficult for him to be deceived. So it is with our familiarity with Christ and his gospel.

In fact, the "elect" are among Satan's highest priority targets. Nephi's discourse on deception goes on to include pointed words aimed directly at warning members of the Church: "And others will he pacify, and lull them away into carnal security, that they will say: All is well in Zion; yea, Zion prospereth, all is well—and thus the devil cheateth their souls, and leadeth them away carefully down to hell" (2 Nephi 28:21).

Those who are in a position to say "all is well in Zion" are those who would have reason to believe they are in Zion in the first place. Indeed, this is a clear warning to the Saints. We are prone to the deception, Nephi says, of being pacified by "carnal security" and prosperity. In other words, we are subject to "the better way" of ignoring and forgetting the Lord when we are focused on our own temporal wealth and financial comforts.

SELF-AWARENESS GROUPS

Some years ago, I was invited by a friend of mine to attend a meeting of a group that was being held across town in the home of a man whom I did not know but who was a highly respected professional in our community. I had no interest whatsoever in attending this meeting, and if it had not been for my friendship and respect for the person who invited me, I would never have gone. It was to be held late at night, and I had to teach early-morning seminary the next morning.

My friend told me that he wanted my opinion on something that he felt had changed his life. He was an experienced priesthood leader and teacher, and we had known each other for years. It intrigued me when he told me obliquely of having his life "changed." I was curious.

When I arrived at the home where the meeting was to be held, I observed that it was a bit like a few of the "cottage meetings" that we had held as missionaries in the homes of members, where they invited their friends to be introduced to the Church. There were eight or nine others there—including more than one member of the Church. As our host began to introduce the evening, he started at one end of the room and invited everyone, one at a time, to talk about how their "program" had "changed their life."

I soon realized that I was the only person in the room who was not part of the "program." It became obvious, as I listened to the "testimonies" of everyone else, that I was the target of this meeting. I was being recruited into a self-awareness program.

The program had a name, which I have long since forgotten. What I have never forgotten is the feeling I had as I sat and listened to those around me talk about how the "program" was responsible for "opening their eyes," for making wonderful, personal "breakthroughs," and for helping them overcome bad habits and putting things behind them that were holding them back. There have been very few occasions in my life where the Spirit of the Lord left me so completely as that night. I couldn't wait to leave. I even passed on the refreshments.

Since that night many years ago, I have had plenty of time to think about what happened to me and why I felt the loss of the Spirit so strongly. I have been prayerful as I have considered this question. Now, I believe I know why my impressions were so strong: The Savior was nowhere to be found in the program. Christ had been replaced. All of the credit for the life-changing events that were recounted by the participants was given to the program. Not to the Savior; not to the Father; but to a program. This was Korihor's strategy in the Book of Mormon: replace the Atonement with the philosophies of men.

Remember the words of Satan as he presented his "better way": "Wherefore, give me thine honor." This is a telling clue to watch for when judging the value of the self-help programs of the world that provide a replacement for repentance. Those alternatives that require us to give honor to anything but the Savior are clear deceptions of Satan.

When we become so "converted" to programs that assist us in making positive change in our lives (and positive change is an outcome that we all would agree is a good thing) that we grant that program too much honor and credit at the expense of recognizing the Savior and His sacrifice, that too is a serious problem. The thirteenth article of faith properly instructs us to seek after things that are "lovely, of good report, or praiseworthy." There are many such worthwhile programs available to assist us in overcoming challenges and trials. An appropriate question is, where is the honor?

I have come to understand that what I witnessed that night was actually a cleverly disguised alternative to the process of repentance. It was a deception, pure and simple. As I read in Moroni, I came to understand better why the Spirit left me that night:

> For behold, the Spirit of Christ is given to every man, that he may know good from evil; wherefore, I show unto you the way to judge; for every thing which inviteth to do good, and to persuade to believe in Christ, is sent forth by the power and gift of Christ; wherefore ye may know with a perfect knowledge it is of God.
>
> But whatsoever thing persuadeth men to do evil, and not believe in Christ, and deny him, and serve not Got, then ye may know with a perfect knowledge it is of the devil; for after this manner doth the devil work, for he persuadeth no man to do good, no, not one; neither do his angels; neither do they who subject themselves unto him.
>
> And now, my brethren, seeing that ye know the light by which ye may judge, which light is the Light of Christ, see that ye do not judge wrongfully; for with that same judgment which ye judge ye shall also be judged.
>
> Wherefore, I beseech of you, brethren, that ye should search diligently in the Light of Christ that ye may know good from evil; and if ye will lay hold upon every good thing, and condemn it not, ye certainly will be a child of Christ. (Moroni 7:16–19)

Satan would have us believe that whenever we make a positive change in our life, it is because of something other than the Savior and His atoning sacrifice. When we do so, we involve ourselves with things that "persuade men not to believe in Christ." We may not do so intentionally, and we may not even realize what we have done. That is how Satan works. That is how he deceives even the elect.

GLORY IN OUR OWN STRENGTH AND WISDOM

We deceive ourselves when we think we overcame our bad habits because we were smart enough, wise enough, and strong enough to finally take charge of our own life. We can take all the credit—which is the essence of pure pride. Basing these personal breakthroughs on pride makes true repentance completely impossible, for repentance requires the humility of a broken heart and contrite spirit. Many self-help programs are entirely centered—or self centered, it could be said—upon this principle. This was one of Korihor's anti-Christ arguments, when he preached that, "every man prospered according to his genius, and that every man conquered according to his strength" (Alma 30:17).

Elder Dallin H. Oaks spoke regarding this deception at the Priesthood Session of the October 2004 general conference, when he said:

> The prophet Nephi warns against another kind of deception: "And others will he pacify, and lull them away into carnal security, that they will say: All is well in Zion; yea, Zion prospereth, all is well—and thus the devil cheateth their souls, and leadeth them away carefully down to hell" (2 Nephi 28:21).
>
> Those who fall for this deception may profess to believe in God, but they do not take His commandments or His justice seriously. They are confident in their own prosperity and conclude that God must have accepted their chosen route.[1]

GLORY IN PHILOSOPHIES OF MEN

We may be led to believe that a seminar or "encounter" group has revealed to us things that we had never supposed, and empowered us to make breakthroughs in our behaviors. Credit goes to some new technology or program. It creates a false Christ, and replaces the true Savior with the philosophies of man.

Again, Elder Oaks taught:

> One kind of deception seeks to mislead us about whom we should follow. In speaking of the last days, the Savior taught: "Take heed that no man deceive you. For many shall come in my name saying, I am Christ; and shall deceive many" (Matthew 24:4–5). In other words, many will seek to deceive us by saying that they or their teachings will save us, so there is no need for a Savior or His gospel. The Book of Mormon describes this as "the power of the devil, to lead away and deceive the hearts of the people . . . to believe that the doctrine of Christ was a foolish and a vain thing" (3 Nephi 2:2).[2]

---

1. Dallin H. Oaks, "Be Not Deceived," *Ensign*, Nov. 2004.
2. Oaks, "Be Not Deceived," *Ensign*.

THE GLORY IN FALSE PROPHETS

We may believe that a self-help book or audio tape series purchased from an infomercial or bookstore has changed our life and given us the strength to master ourselves. To become immersed in such philosophies frequently leads followers to accept false representatives of a false gospel. Credit for any positive change goes to the "guru" who is the personality behind the slick marketing of the materials, as evidenced by scores of personal attestations made by celebrities and sports figures who also credit the guru with their successes. The celebrity endorsements are used as marketing tools for the sole purpose of attracting those who seek to emulate that celebrity status. This is a dangerous trap, for it replaces Christ as the proper object of our emulation with things of the world.

The Book of Mormon describes this type of activity as priestcraft: "He commandeth that there shall be no priestcrafts; for, behold, priestcrafts are that men preach and set themselves up for a light unto the world, that they may get gain and praise of the world; but they seek not the welfare of Zion. Behold the Lord hath forbidden this thing . . . for if they labor for money they shall perish" (2 Nephi 26:29–31).

The deception of false prophets is not always intentional, however. Many have experienced or seen the consequences of new Church members being converted to the missionaries who taught them, instead of to the Savior. Even more seasoned Saints may fall prey to the same deception, becoming converted to a dynamic and effective bishop or stake president. Sadly, when this occurs and the missionaries are transferred or the bishop is eventually released, the members who never became converted to Christ are also left without a gospel of salvation.

Each of these examples—and there are many others—represents "a better way." They are Satan's alternatives to the true principle of repentance. Many who immerse themselves in these alternatives report many positive changes in their life. While those positive changes may be real, they have been ultimately nonetheless deceived. Forgiveness does not come at the end of a seminar or audio book series. It only comes through the true gospel of repentance.

Because of the experience I had as a recruit for a self-awareness group, I was personally relieved and pleased when the First Presidency sent the following letter, dated 21 June 1999, to priesthood leaders in the United States and Canada:

We again remind Church members to be cautious in seeking help from groups that purport to increase self-awareness, raise self-esteem, or enhance individual agency. Some such groups falsely claim or imply Church endorsement. Some charge exorbitant fees or encourage long-term commitments. Some intermingle worldly concepts with gospel principles in ways that can undermine spirituality and faith. We call your attention to guidelines regarding self-awareness groups found in the Church Handbook of Instructions, page 157, and reprinted on the reverse side of this letter (see Self-Awareness Group Guidelines, reprinted below).

There is usually no quick solution to social or emotional difficulties. Those who suffer from such difficulties should exercise great care in choosing appropriate professionals to assist them. As always, members may consult with priesthood leaders for guidance in identifying sources of help that are fully consistent with gospel principles.

Ward and branch councils should consider carefully whether members in their units are being drawn into such groups. If so, the bishop or branch president should take necessary steps to acquaint these members with the foregoing principles and enclosed guidelines. Where appropriate, the guidelines may be published in ward/branch bulletins. Bishops and branch presidents should use them in counseling members as they deem advisable.

SELF-AWARENESS GROUP GUIDELINES

Church members should not participate in groups that:

1. Challenge religious and moral values or advocate unwarranted confrontation with spouse or family members as a means of reaching one's potential.
2. Imitate sacred rites or ceremonies.
3. Foster physical contact among participants.
4. Meet late into the evening or in the early-morning hours.
5. Encourage open confession or disclosure of personal information normally discussed only in confidential settings.
6. Cause a husband and wife to be paired with other partners.[3]

Clearly this does not mean that every support group or self-help group is evil or of the devil. There are a number of groups that offer

---

3. "News of the Church," *Ensign,* Dec. 1999, 70.

emotional support and guidance to individuals who struggle with many challenges. The Church has worked with and assisted several of these support programs to assist people through the practical aspects of such things as overcoming addictive behaviors, for example.

My point is that as members of The Church of Jesus Christ of Latter-day Saints, who have entered into the everlasting covenant—or the covenant of the Atonement—through the waters of baptism, we simply cannot allow the Savior to be replaced in our lives by the doctrine of man. We cannot allow ourselves to be led to believe—or even entertain the thought—that our salvation comes as the result of Alcoholics Anonymous, Overeaters Anonymous, Shoplifters Anonymous, or any other twelve-step program or self-awareness or "encounter" group—no matter how valuable, effective, or good-intentioned they are. Salvation only comes through Jesus Christ; and only faith, repentance, baptism, and the gift of the Holy Ghost open for us access to the mercies and grace of His atoning sacrifice. "Yea, behold I say unto you, that as these things are true, and as the Lord God liveth, there is none other name given under heaven save it be this Jesus Christ, of which I have spoken, whereby man can be saved" (2 Nephi 25:20).

"And now, behold, my beloved brethren, this is the way; and there is none other way nor name given under heaven whereby man can be saved in the kingdom of God. And now this is the doctrine of Christ, and the only and true doctrine of the Father, and of the Son, and of the Holy Ghost, which is one God, without end, Amen" (2 Nephi 31:21). We must be extremely wary. Satan seeks to have us and will stop at nothing within his power to destroy our souls. The prophets have warned us with good reason that some of the programs of the world "intermingle worldly concepts with gospel principles in ways that can undermine spirituality and faith." We must be careful to be forewarned, warn our neighbor, and heed the wisdom and counsel of our Church leaders regarding these things: "whether by mine own voice or by the voice of my servants, it is the same" (D&C 1:38).

Elder Oaks concluded his remarks on this subject during the 2004 General Conference with the following words of warning and instruction:

> The Holy Ghost will protect us against being deceived, but to realize that wonderful blessing, we must always do the things necessary to retain that Spirit. We must keep the commandments,

pray for guidance, and attend church and partake of the sacrament each Sunday. And we must never do anything to drive away that Spirit. Specifically, we should avoid pornography, alcohol, tobacco and drugs, and always, always avoid violations of the law of chastity. We must never take things into our bodies or do things with our bodies that drive away the Spirit of the Lord and leave us without our spiritual protection against deception.

I will conclude by describing another subtle form of deception—the idea that it is enough to hear and believe without acting on that belief. Many prophets have taught against that deception. The Apostle James wrote, "Be ye doers of the word, and not hearers only, deceiving your own selves" (James 1:22). King Benjamin taught, "And now, if you believe all these things see that ye do them" (Mosiah 4:10). And in modern revelation the Lord declares, "If you will that I give unto you a place in the celestial world, you must prepare yourselves by doing the things which I have commanded and required of you" (D&C 78:7).

It is not enough to know that God lives, that Jesus Christ is our Savior, and that the gospel is true. We must take the high road by acting upon that knowledge. It is not enough to know that President Gordon B. Hinckley is God's prophet. We must put his teachings to work in our lives. It is not enough to have a calling. We must fulfill our responsibilities. The things taught in this conference are not just to fill our minds. They are to motivate and guide our actions.[4]

Occasionally, we may find it necessary to prune things from our lives that distract us from our eternal goals. These distractions take many forms which may, from all appearances, have no obvious negative implications. Indeed, some of the things that most distract us may have some inherent benefits. But, when we recognize that these things—whatever they are—are keeping us from progressing, repenting, worshipping and knowing Christ; when we see that we have started to worship the god of youth soccer, musical theatre, sports and competition, wealth, karate class, television, vanity, or whatever distracts us from things of the eternities, it is time to make some dramatic decisions. These are tough decisions because they may require us to set aside things that could be thought of as adding benefits to our life. However, sometimes those "benefits" come at too great a cost. Consider the words of the Savior: "Wherefore if thy hand or thy foot offend

---

4. Oaks, "Be Not Deceived," *Ensign.*

thee, cut them off and cast them from thee: it is better for thee to enter into life halt or maimed, rather than having two hands or two feet to be cast into everlasting fire" (Matthew 18:8).

As we hold fast to the standard works and the words of the prophets and apostles, we will be prepared to protect our families and defend gospel truths from the deceptions of Satan. As we learn to recognize the Savior through our repentance and obedience, we can become steadfast in our ability to withstand these deceptions.

CHAPTER SEVEN

Councils of Repentance

O then, my beloved brethren, repent ye, and enter in at the strait gate, and continue in the way which is narrow, until ye shall obtain eternal life.

—*Jacob 6:11*

WHEN SEEKING FORGIVENESS FROM OUR HEAVENLY FATHER, IT is necessary in some instances that we counsel with those whom the Lord has designated to ensure that every needful thing has been properly attended to in order that our repentance is complete and full. With the proper humility, contrition, and perspective, this opportunity should be welcomed and anticipated. Unfortunately, however, the circumstances surrounding sin often create an environment in which a disciplinary council is a dreaded and annoying consequence to significant disobedience. The difference between one scenario and the other is solely determined by the attitude of the person for whom the council is called.

These councils can be called by those who are set apart as judges in Israel: stake presidents, bishops, mission presidents, district presidents, or branch presidents. The specific circumstances of the situation determine which of these leaders initiate and preside over the proceedings. For the sisters in the Church, the unendowed, those that hold the Aaronic Priesthood, and for Melchizedek Priesthood holders involved in sin not likely to result in excommunication, the responsibility to call and preside over disciplinary councils falls to the bishop. For Melchizedek Priesthood holders involved in sin that has a more-likely-than-not chance of resulting in excommunication, the stake president calls the council and presides.

A bishop's council is generally less complex than a stake president's council, if only for the fact that fewer people are directly involved. A bishop's council consists of the bishopric, with the bishop presiding.

In the Doctrine and Covenants, we find that the Lord has revealed a great deal about the operation and procedures of these councils under the direction of the stake president. Section 102 of the Doctrine and Covenants contains detailed instruction as to how these disciplinary councils function. These verses describe the function of the stake presidency in these proceedings, as well as the role of the high council. Great care is given to provide a setting in which the council acts in love and concern for the welfare of the individual in a balanced and even-handed way. The revelation provides for fully half of the high council to prevent an atmosphere of injustice against the accused. The testimony is given, the matter is discussed, and the decision is made by the president and sustained by the high council:

> The president of the Church, who is also the president of the council, is appointed by revelation, and acknowledged in his administration by the voice of the Church. And it is according to the dignity of his office that he should preside over the council of the Church; and it is his privilege to be assisted by two other presidents, appointed after the same manner that he himself was appointed. And in case of the absence of one or both of those who are appointed to assist him, he has power to preside over the council without an assistant; and in case he himself is absent, the other presidents have power to preside in his stead, both or either of them.
>
> Whenever a high council of the Church of Christ is regularly organized, according to the foregoing pattern, it shall be the duty of the twelve councilors to cast lots by numbers, and thereby ascertain who of the twelve shall speak first, commencing with number one and so in succession to number twelve. Whenever this council convenes to act upon any case, the twelve councilors shall consider whether it is a difficult one or not; if it is not, two only of the councilors shall speak upon it, according to the form above written. But if it is thought to be difficult, four shall be appointed; and if more difficult six; but in no case shall more than six be appointed to speak.
>
> The accused, in all cases, has a right to one-half of the council, to prevent insult or injustice. And the councilors appointed to speak before the council are to present the case, after the evidence is examined, in its true light before the council; and every man is to speak according to the equity of justice. Those councilors who draw even numbers, that is, 2, 4, 6, 8, 10, and 12, are the individuals who are to stand up in behalf of the accused, and prevent insult and injustice.

In all cases, the accuser and the accused shall have a privilege of speaking for themselves before the council, after the evidences are heard and the councilors who are appointed to speak on the case have finished their remarks. After the evidences are heard, the councilors, accuser and accused have spoken, the president shall give a decision according to the understanding which he shall have of the case, and call upon the twelve councilors to sanction the same by their vote. (D&C 102:9–18)

The revelation goes on to discuss additional details pertaining to the decision-making procedure as well as the appeals process. I find it comforting that these matters were provided by the Lord so early in the Restoration of His Church on the earth and these things were not left to the wisdom of man to develop through trial and error over the years. Certainly He knew that there was simply too much at stake in the life of the individual in matters of Church discipline and repentance to risk leaving these councils to leaders without guidance, instruction, and direction. Today, bishops and stake presidents also have significant additional guidance on these matters from the First Presidency and provided in the General Handbook of Instructions.

Formerly known as "Church courts," the proper current designation is a "disciplinary council." A disciplinary council finds its root in the term "discipline," which is based on a word with which we are familiar: disciple. In our context the term "disciple" connotes a follower of our Lord and Savior, Jesus Christ. Disciplinary councils help us follow Christ.

THE NATURE OF DISCIPLINE

The word "discipline" has several meanings that we may find edifying:

1. Training to improve strength or self-control
2. The act of punishing; "The offenders deserved the harsh discipline they received"
3. The trait of being well behaved; "He insisted on discipline among the troops"
4. A system of rules of conduct of method of practice; "For such a plan to work requires discipline"
5. A branch of knowledge; "In what discipline is his doctorate?"
6. Train by instruction and practice; to teach self-control; "Parents must discipline their children"

Application of several of these definitions to the concept of the disciplinary councils of the Church can be very useful. While these councils are always councils of love and generally councils of repentance, they may also properly be considered as councils of "training to improve strength or self-control"; councils of "rules of conduct and method of practice" of the gospel of Jesus Christ; councils of "being well behaved"; councils of "a branch of knowledge" of the gospel; and councils of training "by instruction and practice" in the principle of repentance.

Sometimes, the Lord may also use these councils as a means of "punishing" those who would harm or damage the Church or those involved in predatory behaviors against the innocent; or as councils of "punishment in order to gain or enforce obedience" to gospel standards and principles. So, the purposes of a disciplinary council are many. This is made clear in the following statement by an Apostle of the Lord:

> Members sometimes ask why Church disciplinary councils are held. The purpose is threefold: first, to save the soul of the transgressor; second, to protect the innocent; and third, to safeguard the Church's purity, integrity and good name.
>
> The First Presidency has instructed that disciplinary councils must be held in cases of murder, incest, apostasy, or advocating and teaching apostate and anti-Church doctrine. In addition to these cases and those involving a prominent Church leader, a disciplinary council must be held when the transgressor is a predator who may be a threat to other persons, when the person shows a pattern of repeated serious transgressions, or when a serious transgression is widely known.
>
> Disciplinary councils are not called to try civil or criminal cases; in fact, criminal charges may or may not necessitate Church discipline. The decision of a civil court may help determine whether a Church disciplinary council should be convened. However, a civil court's decision does not dictate the decision of a disciplinary council.
>
> Disciplinary councils are not held for such things as failure to pay tithing, to obey the Word of Wisdom, to attend church, or to receive home teachers. They are not held because of business failure or nonpayment of debts. They are not designed to settle disputes among members. Nor are they held for members who demand that

their names be removed from the Church records, unless a member who has committed a serious transgression is requesting name removal to avoid the possibility of excommunication or disfellowshipment. The removal of a person's name from the records of the Church is a very serious step, but is handled as an administrative action.[1]

I have participated in disciplinary councils from three different perspectives, each of which have taught me a great deal. First, I have participated as the presiding authority, with responsibility to ensure that the actions and spirit of the council is in accordance with the scriptures and instruction from the First Presidency. Second, I have participated as a member of the council, with responsibility to feel of the proper spirit, and to ensure that appropriate and sufficient questions were asked and answered to allow me to sustain the decision of the presiding officer without reservation. Third, I have attended disciplinary councils as the non-participating priesthood leader of the person for whom the council was called, to lend support and comfort, where I have watched and empathized with the men of the council as they sought diligently and earnestly to arrive at an understanding of their Heavenly Father's will.

In these roles, and from these different perspectives, I have come to appreciate the spirit of love that permeates these councils. They truly are councils of love. I have witnessed and been party to the shedding of many tears in those settings. Priesthood leaders who have responsibility to participate as members of a disciplinary council do so with feelings of charity, empathy, understanding, and soberness. While I am aware of some priesthood leaders who express dread at the thought of participating in a disciplinary council, I have always—in every single instance—left a disciplinary council strengthened deeply by the spirit of the proceedings and recommitted to a greater degree of personal righteousness and obedience in my own life. I have always left with gratitude in my heart for my wife and family, for the blessings of the gospel of Jesus Christ and His atoning sacrifice.

Those who participate in disciplinary councils consider carefully not only the facts of the particular case before them but also the surrounding

1. M. Russel Ballard, *Counseling with Our Councils: Learning to Minister to One Another in the Church and in the Family,* (Salt Lake City: Deseret Book, 1997) 138–139.

circumstances that may be mediating or condemning in nature. It is a serious and sacred responsibility that I have never seen taken lightly. Again from Elder Ballard:

> The council takes into consideration many factors, such as whether temple or marriage covenants have been violated; whether a position of trust or authority has been abused; the repetition, seriousness, and magnitude of the transgression; the age, maturity, and experience of the transgressor; the interests of innocent victims and innocent family members; the time between transgression and confession; whether or not confession was voluntary; and evidence of repentance.
>
> Those who sit on the council are to keep everything strictly confidential and to handle the matter in a spirit of love. That includes being respectful and dignified throughout the disciplinary process. . . . Remember, the objective of the council is not retribution; it is to help the member make the changes necessary to stand clean before God once more. Those who come before any Church disciplinary council are entitled to be treated with respect and courtesy.[2]

INDIVIDUAL TREATMENT OF SIMILAR SINS

Perhaps there are some who have felt that Church disciplinary councils have been inconsistent in treating different individuals who have committed similar offenses. There are no iron-clad rules or "mandatory sentencing guidelines" for any sins other than murder and most cases of incest. In every other instance, the council has latitude to make the decision that is dictated by the Spirit. I have come to learn that the overriding principle in that decision is usually to impose the minimum amount of discipline that will result in full and complete repentance by the individual.

Understandably, different individuals who have committed similar sins—even two different parties to the same action—may require different degrees of discipline to achieve the results that the Lord desires. For that reason, in addition to the fact that councils will have access to information and circumstances that will not be publicly known, it is important for those not directly involved in a particular disciplinary council to not make an outside judgment about the results.

---

2.   Ballard, *Counseling with Our Councils,* 140.

On one occasion, as I presided as bishop over a disciplinary council, my counselors and I had the experience—the only time this has occurred to me—when at the conclusion of hearing testimony, asking and receiving answers to questions, and private deliberation, we experienced such a mutual "stupor of thought" over the matter that we were for some time entirely confused as to the proper course for us to take. In every other previous experience I had with my counselors in similar circumstances, the Spirit manifested the proper decision unanimously to us by the end of our deliberations. We then would take the matter to the Lord for confirmation, which was always received in unmistakable terms.

This time, however, we had no such immediate understanding of the Lord's will in the matter. Having no other place to go for guidance, we knelt together in prayer, seeking to know what decision should be made to assist this member in the course of repentance and in obtaining forgiveness. As we did so, the Spirit revealed to each of us, independently of each other, a clear and distinct impression and understanding of what should be done. When we closed our prayer, opened our eyes, and looked at each other, I knew that they knew as well as I did what the Lord had made manifest in the matter. There was no further confusion and no need for additional discussion. The decision had been made and was given to us from above.

I shall never forget the experience we had of receiving what I can only term as a united revelation on the matter. I know that God is involved in the proceedings of the disciplinary councils of the Church. I also know that the decisions made in these councils are made in love and empathy, with prayer and a desire for the eternal salvation of the individual's soul.

CHAPTER EIGHT

Man's Agency

Abide ye in the liberty wherewith ye are made free; entangle not yourselves in sin, but let your hands be clean, until the Lord comes.

—*Doctrine and Covenants 88:86*

THE ROLE OF AGENCY IN THE NEW AND everlasting covenant is such a fundamental and simple doctrine that it is difficult to understand how it can be so widely misunderstood. And yet, I have found in counseling with many youth—and their parents—that it is a doctrine frequently misunderstood and mistaught in our homes. Agency is essential for the salvation of man. Without agency, God's purposes would fail, for we would be incapable of achieving eternal life. Because the principle of agency is such a basic, foundational doctrine, if we fail to understand it or teach it properly, the results can be catastrophic.

Several years ago, I sat with the father and mother of one of the youth in the ward. They had come to the bishop's office at my request. I had been experiencing strong feelings of unease—even alarm—about their child, and I felt that I needed to counsel with these parents regarding my concerns. There were many early indicators of high-risk behavior suddenly apparent in the child, and I simply could not get this child out of my mind. I had also noticed a significant change in the countenance and demeanor of this child in recent weeks. I shared my feelings, my concerns, and warnings with the parents and sought to find a way to assist them in bringing their child back toward the Savior.

I will never forget what the father told me that night. He said, "Bishop, [the child] has [his or her] free agency. What can we do? Didn't

Joseph Smith say that we should teach our children correct principles and let them govern themselves?" That perspective has haunted me ever since.

Unfortunately, too many parents and far too many children misunderstand the principle of agency just as that father did. And what they think they understand about the way agency works is largely a false doctrine—another of Satan's slick deceptions or half-truths. I have spent a lot of time in Sunday School and priesthood classes over the years listening to lessons and discussions about so-called "free agency," as if it really is "free"—like the Resurrection is—or as if it is a license for us to have the "freedom" to do with as we please.

Agency is not free. It never has been. The greatest of all prices ever paid was paid for our agency. Agency cost the Father a full one-third of his spirit sons and daughters—even before a single soul could be lost to earthly sin. The Savior had to pay the price for all of the combined consequences of all the wrong choices of all God's children in order that we might have our agency on earth. We cannot begin to fathom the price that has been paid for our agency!

The War in Heaven was fought over agency. Lucifer rebelled against God, "became Satan," and was cast out of the first estate because he "sought to destroy the agency of man, which I the Lord God, had given him" (Moses 4:3–4). Satan continues that very same battle here on earth, waged with the assistance of those who followed him.

SATAN'S PRIMARY WEAPON

"And behold, others he flattereth away, and telleth them there is no hell; and he saith unto them: I am no devil, for there is none—and thus he whispereth in their ears, until he grasps them with his awful chains from whence there is no deliverance" (2 Nephi 28:22). Satan's primary weapon is very simple. It can be used with frightening subtlety and alarming appeal. Without even trying to look for it, we see it surrounding us everywhere. He pummels us with it continually from every possible angle. We cannot read a newspaper, a magazine, or watch a television show without being hammered with it. Madison Avenue has made billions of dollars with it once it learned how to harness its tremendous power. It has seeped into every crevice and crack in our society. It successfully targets not only the wicked and ungodly but also the very elect, the fathers and mothers in Zion.

His best weapon is the beguiling lie that there are no consequences. The scriptures teach this principle also, emphasizing the temptation to follow those who preach this false and dangerous doctrine: "But behold, if a man shall come among you and shall say: Do this, and there is no iniquity; do that and ye shall not suffer; yea he will say: Walk after the pride of your own hearts; yea, walk after the pride of your eyes, and do whatsoever your heart desireth—and if a man shall come among you and say this, ye will receive him, and say that he is a prophet" (Helaman 13:27).

Satan would have us believe that we can do what we please, when we please. He assures us that, ultimately, it will not matter because there are no consequences. He parades the unrestrained indulgence in sexuality, violence, and abuse as if it is the only part of the cause/effect relationship that actually exists. He tells us that we can avoid consequences to our actions if they are uncomfortable, ill-timed, or inconvenient. He leads us to believe that no one will ever know what we do in private, so naturally it is not possible for ultimate consequences to exist. This has always been the primary argument of the anti-Christs.

He has many variations on this theme: there is no God; there are no commandments; gospel ordinances are meaningless traditions; the need for a Savior and Redeemer is pure fantasy; Jesus was not a real person; Jesus was a real person, but he was only a teacher; Jesus was not the Son of God; there was no Resurrection of Jesus Christ, and there will be no resurrection of the dead; there are no prophets; there was no War in Heaven; there is no heaven; Satan is not real but is a figment of imagination; the family unit is merely the result of social engineering and natural selection and is not designed by God; "inspiration" is only self-deception; we only live life once, so we should experience everything that life has to offer; life is not sacred but merely the result of biological evolution; the sexual union is intended to be used for our pleasure whenever we please and with whomever we choose; our path in life is predetermined—we are predestined to do what we will do in this life, and so forth. Satan will tell us that a belief and faith in God is only a crutch for the weak, thereby dismissing all eternal blessings and consequences.

By repeating and promoting these deceptions, Satan carefully leads our souls down to hell.

We see this tool of Satan firmly entrenched in our instant-gratification-oriented popular culture. Get chiseled abs without exercise! Lose thirty pounds in seven days! Dealing with an unwanted pregnancy? Have bad credit? Fighting a hangover? Harassed by creditors? Can't control your temper? Feeling down? With all of these circumstances, and many more, we are told that through the magic of medicine or some other simple solution, we can simply take a pill or engage in some other indulgence and the consequences of our behavior will miraculously disappear.

We spend more than we earn, buy expensive items with "no payment until next year," go deeply into debt, and then file bankruptcy and walk away from it all. Small wonder that we come to subconsciously believe over time that Satan's doctrine is true, that there really are no consequences to our actions.

The father and mother who came to my office that night believed within themselves, and had taught their children, that "there was nothing they could do"—that there were no consequences to behavior, only "freedom to choose." This is not what the scriptures teach about agency.

The doctrine of agency requires the presence of five elements or principles:

First, there must be laws or commandments that can either be obeyed or disobeyed. This element was present when our first parents were placed in the Garden of Eden. The first law was given to them when "the Lord God, commanded the man, saying: Of every tree of the garden thou mayest freely eat, but of the tree of the knowledge of good and evil, thou shalt not eat of it" (Moses 3:16–17).

Second, there must be an opposition to the laws or commandments. The scriptures teach the importance of the existence of opposition. Indeed, opposition defines existence:

> For it must needs be, that there is an opposition in all things. If not so . . . righteousness could not be brought to pass, neither wickedness, neither holiness nor misery, neither good nor bad. Wherefore, all things must needs be a compound in one; wherefore, if it should be one body it must needs remain as dead, having no life neither death, nor corruption nor incorruption, happiness nor misery, neither sense nor insensibility.
>
> Wherefore, it must needs have been created for a thing of

naught; wherefore there would have been no purpose in the end of its creation. (2 Nephi 2:11–12)

Third, those who are to exercise agency must have knowledge of good and evil—or in other words, intelligence must be present: "All truth is independent in that sphere in which God has placed it, to act for itself, as all intelligence also; otherwise there is no existence. Behold, here is the agency of man, and here is the condemnation of man; because that which was from the beginning is plainly manifest unto them, and they receive not the light" (D&C 93:30–31).

Fourth, the power of choice must prevail. Immediately upon receiving the commandment from the Lord, Adam and Eve were then told, "nevertheless, thou mayest choose for thyself, for it is given unto thee" (Moses 3:17).

Fifth, there must be consequences to choice: blessings for obedience and penalties for disobedience. Adam and Eve were given clear instruction regarding the consequences to disobedience when the Lord said, "but, remember that I forbid it, for in the day thou eatest thereof thou shalt surely die" (Moses 3:17). Consequence as an essential element of agency is also taught in the Doctrine and Covenants: "That every man may act in doctrine and principle pertaining to futurity, according to the moral agency which I have given unto him, that every man may be accountable for his own sins in the day of judgment" (D&C 101:78).

Adam and Eve were free to make a choice, but they were not free to escape the consequence. Nor could they bargain for a better deal. God told them in no uncertain terms that "in the day thou eatest thereof thou shalt surely die." And they did. Adam and Eve first suffered a spiritual death as they were evicted from the Garden and cast out of God's presence; and second, mortality became an unavoidable consequence for them and their posterity. Other scriptures demonstrate clearly the need for consequences as a gravely fundamental eternal principle. For instance, Alma taught Corianton that "there is a law given, and a punishment affixed"; otherwise, he said, "God would cease to be God" (Alma 42:22).

Of these five elements, which are necessary for agency to exist, the parents I spoke with that night several years ago had forgotten to teach some important—even vital—principles. Yes, they had established "a law" in their home, relatively consistent with gospel standards, and "opposition" was inherently present. Freedom to choose was also clearly provided to the children.

However, as we discussed the challenges they had in their home, it became apparent that little attempt had been made to actually "teach correct principles," leaving their children ill-prepared to "govern themselves" by making the proper choices. It was assumed that correct principles would be somehow magically absorbed by their children through sporadic exposure to Church programs and classes. The gospel of Jesus Christ was not being actively taught in the home; it was instead being passively assumed. They had practically no family home evenings or family prayer. Family and personal scripture study was unheard of. Could they—or we—expect children to make "intelligent" choices without the necessary knowledge and instruction? Of course not.

Moreover, they had fallen prey to Satan's greatest weapon. There were no consequences being taught or enforced in their home. The children had learned a false lesson about the principle of agency, and the parents had "ceased to be parents" in a very essential responsibility.

Our Heavenly Father grants us the exercise of agency using the same five principles. We have been given laws and commandments. We deal with continual opposition to those commandments. We should seek to have knowledge and intelligence so we can make the wise choice. We are allowed to choose as we see fit. And finally, we face the consequences of our choices and actions, and either receive the blessings that are predicated upon the commandments, or live our lives without the presence of those blessings.

"There is a law, irrevocably decreed in heaven before the foundation of this world, upon which all blessings are predicated—and when we obtain any blessing from God, it is by obedience to that law upon which it is predicated" (D&C 130:20–21). However, let us not confuse the principle of consequence with the dark instrument of compulsion. President Howard W. Hunter taught that agency is so fundamentally sacred to God that compulsion is a violation of His very essence:

> To fully understand this gift of agency, and its inestimable worth, it is imperative that we understand that God's chief way of acting is by persuasion, and patience and long-suffering, not by coercion and stark confrontation. He acts by gentle solicitation and sweet enticement. He always acts with unfailing respect for the freedom and independence that we possess. He wants to help us and

pleads for the chance to assist us, but he will not do so in violation of our agency. He loves us too much to do that, and doing so would run counter to his divine nature.[1]

Indeed, why would God take away the very agency that Christ has paid the ultimate price to secure? We are not compelled to make the proper choice. In fact, compulsion is a tool of Satan. The blessings of the gospel cannot be forced upon us. We must—as the sacramental prayers point to—be willing to keep the commandments. When we speak of "freedom of choice," we are really talking about being free to be willing servants of God or to be unwilling to serve. We are free to choose the consequences we will face by virtue of our willing obedience or our willful rebellion to the commandments.

> Wherefore, men are free according to the flesh; and all things are given them which are expedient unto man. And they are free to choose liberty and eternal life, through the great Mediator of all men, or to choose captivity and death, according to the captivity and power of the devil; for he seeketh that all men might be miserable like unto himself. (2 Nephi 2:27)

> Therefore, O my son, whosoever will come may come and partake of the waters of life freely; and whosoever will not come the same is not compelled to come; but in the last day it shall be restored unto him according to his deeds. (Alma 42:27)

> And now remember, remember, my brethren, that whosoever perisheth, perisheth unto himself; and whosoever doeth iniquity, doeth it unto himself; for behold, ye are free; ye are permitted to act for yourselves; for behold, God hath given you knowledge and he hath made you free. (Helaman 14:30)

Our exercise of agency determines not only the path of our life, the blessings we will experience, and the detours and setbacks we must endure because of our sins, but it also determines who we ultimately become. When Joseph Smith received the revelation known as the eighty-eighth section of the Doctrine and Covenants, it contained an interesting insight into how our choices affect who we are.

In verses twenty-eight and twenty-nine of section eighty-eight of

---

1. *The Teachings of Howard W. Hunter, Fourteenth President of the Church of Jesus Christ of Latter-day Saints,* (Salt Lake City: Deseret Book, 1997) 78–79.

the Doctrine and Covenants, we learn that those who are of a celestial spirit will be quickened with a celestial body and celestial glory. Verse thirty tells us the same thing as it relates to the terrestrial glory. Those who receive a telestial glory are discussed in verse thirty-one. Then we find this interesting verse: "And they who remain shall also be quickened; nevertheless, they shall return again to their own place, to enjoy that which they are willing to receive, because they were not willing to enjoy that which they might have received" (D&C 88:32).

It seems difficult for us to understand how it is possible that there will be those who will refuse to receive even a telestial glory and who will instead "return again to their own place, to enjoy that which they are willing to receive." Those who "return again to their own place" will do so because that is the type of person that has resulted from their exercise of agency here on earth.

Not everyone will be willing to receive the celestial kingdom and the celestial glory. For, with the highest degree of celestial glory comes exaltation, or "all that my Father hath" (D&C 84:38). Intrinsic to exaltation are the responsibilities of godhood, consisting of ultimate and eternal service to others: bringing to pass the immortality and eternal life of man.

If we have not exercised our agency here on earth in such a way that has allowed us to learn to love being in service to our fellowmen while in mortality, what makes us think that we will be willing to undertake such a responsibility for the eternities while in immortality? In a real and eternal sense, we become the person we choose to become. It is not an outcome forced upon us against our will or our agency. It is the final, absolute, and ultimate freedom of choice. "For what doth it profit a man if a gift is bestowed upon him, and he receive not the gift? Behold, he rejoices not in that which is given unto him, neither rejoices in him who is the giver of the gift" (D&C 88:33).

A THEORY FROM THE BOOK OF REVELATION

One morning when I was serving as a full-time missionary in Singapore, my companion and I were studying the New Testament together in the book of Revelation. I have always struggled with Revelation. The symbolism is a real challenge for me even now. As young missionaries, my companion and I developed a theory about the interpretation of a verse in Revelation chapter twelve that I have found useful in my understanding of agency—acknowledging the fact that our speculation may not necessarily be the proper interpretation (and certainly isn't the only interpretation) of the specific scripture.

Revelation chapter twelve talks about a vision John the Revelator received concerning the Apostasy of the Church. It also addresses the War in Heaven and Satan's continued war here on earth. Agency is at the core of all the events discussed in this chapter. A discussion of our theory and interpretation is found Appendix A.

According to my mission-inspired theory, the last thread of true Christianity was lost when agency was restricted by apostasy. The War in Heaven over the agency of man was continued on the earth, and when Satan held sufficient power over the hearts of men that agency could no longer be defended and upheld on the earth by the power of the priesthood, the Apostasy began. The darkest ages of human history occurred when the agency of man was very limited in every way.

The laws and commandments of God were not only subject to the interpretations of men during the Apostasy, but they were also used as tools of political abuse by rulers and leaders that claimed to either have authority from God or claimed to be deity. Without the power of the priesthood on the earth, the light and knowledge that enlightens the intellect of man was greatly diminished. There was no power of choice in religious matters. The Bibles were chained to the pulpits and the reading of the scriptures—even by the priests—was considered to be a suspicious thing. For a long while on the earth, the gospel of Satan prevailed.

The Restoration of the gospel of Jesus Christ required an environment that would support freedom and the exercise of agency. This was not an easy, smooth, or quick process. Historians have written a great deal on the revival of learning that occurred in human history as the renaissance bloomed, ushering in resurgence in navigation, engineering, agriculture, a desire burning in men's hearts to contact other horizons, continents and peoples, and a dissemination of knowledge and thought through the printed word.

Inspired men such as John Wycliffe in England, John Huss in Bohemia, and Martin Luther in Germany served as instruments in the Lord's hands in preparing the world to be able to defend and uphold agency on the earth again. The leaven they provided to the world caught hold and the "Reformation" was firmly established in much of

Western Europe. However, the reformers were limited because they did had not have the gift of the Holy Ghost.

Nephi saw these circumstances in vision and recorded them in 1 Nephi, chapter thirteen. As we read the words of Nephi, we find many subtle references to the role agency—or the limitation on it—played in the Apostasy and Restoration:

> And it came to pass that I saw among the nations of the Gentiles the formation of a great church.
>
> And the angel said unto me: Behold the formation of a church which is most abominable above all other churches, which slayeth the saints of God, yea, and tortureth them and bindeth them down and yoketh them with a yoke of iron, and bringeth them down into captivity.
>
> And it came to pass that I beheld this great and abominable church; and I saw the devil that he was the founder of it. . . .
>
> And also for the praise of the world do they destroy the saints of God, and bring them down into captivity. (1 Nephi 13:4–7, 9)

Then, Nephi saw the creation of a new nation on a promised land delivered by the power of God that would offer protection to those who would be led to it:

> And I looked and beheld a man among the Gentiles, who was separated from the seed of my brethren by the many waters; and I beheld the Spirit of God, that it came down and wrought upon the man; and he went forth upon the many waters, even unto the seed of my brethren, who were in the promised land.
>
> And it came to pass that I beheld the Spirit of God, that it wrought upon other Gentiles; and they went forth out of captivity, upon the many waters. . . .
>
> And it came to pass that I, Nephi, beheld that the Gentiles who had gone forth out of captivity did humble themselves before the Lord; and the power of the Lord was with them.
>
> And I beheld that their mother Gentiles were gathered together upon the waters, and upon the land also, to battle against them.
>
> And I beheld that the power of God was with them, and also that the wrath of God was upon all those that were gathered together against them to battle.
>
> And I, Nephi, beheld that the Gentiles that had gone out of captivity were delivered by the power of God out of the hands of all other nations. (1 Nephi 13:12–13, 16–19)

This new country offered to the Gentiles freedom from captivity. Or, in other words, with the creation of this new country—itself freed from its "mother" country, an environment of agency could be cultivated that would offer the exercise of choice sufficient to sustain the Restoration of Christ's Church to the earth. Nephi writes that it was a land provided by covenant, which gives it added significance in the context of the principles discussed in this book: "Nevertheless, thou beholdest that the Gentiles who have gone forth out of captivity, and have been lifted up by the power of God above all other nations, upon the face of the land which is choice above all other lands, which is the land that the Lord God hath covenanted with thy father that his seed should have for the land of their inheritance" (1 Nephi 13:30).

The United States declared independence in 1776 and subsequently fought in the Revolutionary War. The colonies that settled in America joined together and formed a Constitution that organized a government based on freedom, which was then adopted in September 1787 and went into effect on March 4, 1789. Of the Constitution of the United States of America, the Lord said:

> And now, verily I say unto you concerning the laws of the land, it is my will that my people should observe to do all things whatsoever I command them.
>
> And that law of the land which is constitutional, supporting the principles of freedom in maintaining rights and privileges, belongs to all mankind, and is justifiable before me.
>
> Therefore, I, the Lord, justify you and your brethren of my church, in befriending that law which is the constitutional law of the land;
>
> And as pertaining to the laws of man, whatever is more or less than this cometh of evil.
>
> I, the Lord God, make you free, therefore ye are free indeed; and the law also maketh you free. (D&C 98:4–8)
>
> That every man may act in doctrine and principle pertaining to futurity, according to the moral agency which I have given unto him, that every man may be accountable for his own sins in the day of judgment.
>
> Therefore, it is not right that any man should be in bondage one to another.
>
> And for this purpose have I established the Constitution of this land, by the hands of wise men whom I raised up unto this very purpose, and redeemed the land by the shedding of blood. (D&C 101:78–80)

In order to sustain and uphold the agency of man to the degree that would be required for this new nation, and for a complete Restoration of the gospel of Jesus Christ to survive, the Lord brought the Gentiles out of their captivity—at a time when their agency was still withheld from them regarding many religious issues—and they were "delivered by the power of God out of the hands of all other nations" to a "promised land," given by covenant. He then "established the Constitution" to make men "free indeed."

From the Declaration of Independence to the implementation of the Constitution, it took approximately thirteen difficult years to truly free themselves. Even then, the conflict with the "mother" country was not fully resolved until the War of 1812—which took another twenty-three years to accomplish.

The Lord was already moving quickly, however. The prophet of the Restoration, Joseph Smith, had already been born in 1805. In 1815, the Smith family moved to Palmyra, near where the golden plates lay buried in the Hill Cumorah. In 1820, Joseph received the First Vision in which he saw God the Father and Jesus Christ and was told not to join any church, for they "draw near to me with their lips, but their hearts are far from me, they teach for doctrines the commandments of men, having the form of godliness, but they deny the power thereof" (JS–H 1:19).

In 1823, Moroni visited Joseph, taught him about many prophesies related to the Restoration of the gospel in the last days, and told him about the golden plates containing a sacred record. He received the plates in 1827 and then commenced with the translation and publication of the Book of Mormon through much tribulation. The priesthood was restored in 1829, and the Church was officially organized on April 6, 1830. The Apostasy was over: the Church had returned from the wilderness that John described in Revelation, and agency—and the power and authority to uphold it—was again on the earth in full.

In retrospect, the Lord moved with remarkable swiftness. Within only forty-one years of the establishment of the Constitution—within the lifetime of many—a prophet had been born, raised up, and had accomplished the work of the Restoration. Through that Prophet, and within that time, the very power and authority of God to administer the laws and ordinances of the new and everlasting covenant had been restored to earth. With the principles of freedom and agency generally protected and in force and the Restoration complete, mankind once again had access to the powers of the atoning sacrifice, to the cleansing powers of repentance and forgiveness through baptism and the exalting covenants and endowments of the temple. The new and everlasting covenant was on the earth again.

CHAPTER NINE

The Doctrine of the Restoration

> Yea this bringeth about the restoration of those things of which has been spoken by the mouths of the prophets.
>
> —*Alma 40:22*

THE SCRIPTURES HAVE ALWAYS PROPHESIED OF A RESTORATION of all things in the last days. Latter-day Saints are understandably sensitive and receptive to those prophesies because of the scriptural basis and support they provide for the Restoration of the gospel through the Prophet Joseph Smith. The establishment of The Church of Jesus Christ of Latter-day Saints is the fulfillment of those prophesies. And yet, it is not the institution of the formal, structural organization of the Church that signaled the end of the Apostasy as much as it was the Restoration of the keys of the priesthood to officiate in the ordinances of the everlasting covenant.

We are generally most familiar with New Testament scriptures pertaining to the Apostasy and Restoration, as well as a few Old Testament references:

> This know also, that in the last days perilous times shall come.
>
> For men shall be lovers of their own selves, covetous, boasters, proud, blasphemers, disobedient to parents, unthankful, unholy,
>
> Without natural affection, trucebreakers, false accusers, incontinent, fierce, despisers of those that are good,
>
> Traitors, heady, highminded, lovers of pleasures more than lovers of God;

Having a form of godliness but denying the power thereof: from such turn away. (2 Timothy 3:1–5)

Now we beseech you, brethren, by the coming of our Lord Jesus Christ, and by our gathering together unto him.

That ye be not soon shaken in mind, or be troubled, neither by spirit, nor by word, nor by letter as from us, as that the day of Christ is at hand.

Let no man deceive you by any means: for that day shall not come, except there come a falling away first, and that man of sin be revealed, the son of perdition;

Who opposeth and exalteth himself above all that is called God, or that is worshipped; so that he as God sitteth in the temple of God, shewing himself that he is God. (2 Thessalonians 2:1–4)

For the time will come when they will not endure sound doctrine; but after their own lusts shall they heap to themselves teachers, having itching ears;

And they shall turn away their ears from the truth, and shall be turned to fables. (2 Timothy 4:3–4)

Behold, the days come, saith the Lord God, that I will send a famine in the land, not a famine of bread, nor a thirst for water, but of hearing the words of the Lord:

And they shall wander from sea to sea, and from the north even to the east, they shall run to and fro to seek the word of the Lord, and shall not find it. (Amos 8:11–12)

And I saw another angel fly in the midst of heaven, having the everlasting gospel to preach unto them that dwell on the earth, and to every nation, and kindred, and tongue, and people,

Saying with a loud voice, Fear God, and give glory to him; for the hour of his judgment is come: and worship him that made heaven, and earth, and the sea, and the fountains of waters. (Revelation 14:6–7)

Repent ye therefore, and be converted, that your sins may be blotted out, when the times of refreshing shall come from the presence of the Lord;

And he shall send Jesus Christ, which before was preached unto you:

Whom the heaven must receive until the times of restitution of all things, which God hath spoken by the mouth of all his holy prophets since the world began. (Acts 3:19–21)

Each of these verses contains remarkable prophesies that have been fulfilled as the world fell into apostasy through the loss of agency, authority, and the everlasting covenant on the earth and the subsequent Restoration of the priesthood and establishment of the Church. Yet, there are other scriptures that make clear that the concept of a restoration is not solely and strictly institutional in nature. There are many personal and private implications to the doctrine of restoration as well. When Peter prophesied of a time of "restitution of all things," I believe he truly meant all things.

We are in dire need of restoration in our lives. As we live in this frail existence, we experience continued loss through sickness, injury, aging, death, victimization, and the consequences of our own sins and the sins of others. Those we have loved may no longer be with us—or may have been taken from us—and we feel a stinging emptiness. Daily tasks that we took for granted in the ease of our youth may now be not challenging but impossible for us in our advancing years. We may have experienced permanent, crippling disease. Our constant exposure to the poisons of Satan, and our knowing or unknowing association with those who follow him, may have robbed us of our ability to trust, reach out to, or rely on others. Failed relationships, soured by consequences of the actions of one or both parties, may leave us bitter and lonely. Poor decisions and bad choices may have left us challenged with the struggles of poverty in the continuing responsibility of caring for ourselves and others. We may have been falsely accused and persecuted and harbor feelings of revenge. Our failure to take advantage of opportunities to improve ourselves may leave us feeling that we have wasted a good portion of our lives.

We could go on and on with frequent and persistent examples of the tragedies of human existence. In each situation, a restoration is urgently needed. It is through the new and everlasting covenant—the atoning sacrifice of Jesus Christ—that such a personal restoration is not only possible but promised. However, the pathway to personal restoration can be a bumpy one, as the teachings of Alma to his son, Corianton, demonstrate.

A MESSAGE FOR CORIANTON

Alma was sent to preach the gospel to an idolatrous and perverted people, the Zoramites. Teaching and converting the Zoramites would be an enormous challenge, and Alma recognized that he would need a small army of dedicated and faithful missionaries to accomplish the work. Leaving one of the sons of Mosiah with the Church in Zara-hemla, Alma took the best he had into the Zoramite mission field: three of the sons of Mosiah, two of his own sons, and two others. In my mind, I picture them as four sets of companionships, with Alma as the mission president:

> Now it came to pass that after the end of Korihor, Alma having received tidings that the Zoramites were perverting the ways of the Lord, and that Zoram, who was their leader, was leading the hearts of the people to bow down to dumb idols, his heart again began to sicken because of the iniquity of the people. (Alma 31:1)

> Therefore he took Ammon, and Aaron, and Omner; and Himni he did leave in the Church in Zarahemla; but the former three he took with him, and also Amulek and Zeezrom, who were at Melek; and he also took two of his sons.
> Now the eldest of his sons he took not with him, and his name was Helaman; but the names of those whom he took with him were Shiblon and Corianton; and these are the names of those who went with him among the Zoramites, to preach unto them the word. (Alma 31:6–7)

Alma must have had a great deal of confidence in Corianton to bring him into association with the Zoramites, who the scriptures describe as "dissenters." Dissenters are particularly insidious and dangerous to weak testimonies because they attack gospel principles from a perspective that includes a background in the culture as well as doctrinal understanding—at some level—of the very teachings they challenge. Alma described dissenters as "having the same instruction and the same information of the Nephites, yea, having been instructed in the same knowledge of the Lord" (Alma 47:36). Dissenters come from within—those we have called our brothers and sisters—not usu-ally from outside the Church. Alma evidently had taken all of this into account in deciding who should accompany him on this spiritually dangerous mission.

We learn from the letters of instruction and counsel Alma wrote to his sons that Corianton fell away and committed grievous sins while he was among the Zoramites. In modern context, he was sent home early and dishonorably released.

And now, my son, I have somewhat more to say unto thee than
what I have said unto thy brother; for behold, have ye not observed
the steadiness of thy brother, his faithfulness, and his diligence in
keeping the commandments of God? Behold, has he not set a good
example for thee?

For thou didst not give so much heed unto my words as did thy
brother, among the people of the Zoramites. Now this is what I have
against thee; thou didst go on unto boasting in thy strength and thy
wisdom.

And this is not all, my son. Thou didst do that which was grievous unto me; for thou didst forsake the ministry, and did go over
into the land of Siron among the borders of the Lamanites, after the
harlot Isabel.

Yea, she did steal away the hearts of many; but this was no
excuse for thee, my son. Thou shouldst have tended to the ministry
wherewith thou wast entrusted. (Alma 39:1–4)

Alma was clearly frustrated, upset, and disappointed with Corianton, and rightfully so. Corianton had caused a great deal of damage.
Not only was his own life a complete mess because of his choices and
actions, but he had caused a lot of damage for his father, the other
missionaries, and among the Zoramites. Alma wrote, "Behold, O my
son, how great iniquity ye brought upon the Zoramites; for when
they saw your conduct they would not believe in my words" (Alma
39:11).

Corianton had created, by his actions, a situation that cried for a
restoration. Alma went on to write to his son some of the clearest and
most beautiful doctrine available to us on the efficacy, requirements,
and impacts of Christ's Atonement. He discusses the realities of the
Resurrection in great detail. He teaches about the Fall of Adam and
the need for a Redeemer. He writes the most detailed and profound
doctrine found in all of the scriptures concerning the relationship
between the principles of justice and mercy. He also teaches Corianton
the doctrine of personal restoration.

The first reference Alma makes to restoration is a physical one,
made in the context of a literal resurrection of the dead:

The soul shall be restored to the body, and the body to the soul;
yea, and every limb and joint shall be restored to its body; yea, even
a hair of the head shall not be lost; but all things shall be restored to
their proper and perfect frame.

> And now, my son, this is the restoration of which has been spoken by the mouths of the prophets—
>
> And then shall the righteous shine forth in the kingdom of God. (Alma 40:23–25)

This discussion addressed concerns that Alma perceived that Corianton had in his mind (see Alma 40:1) but perhaps did not necessarily address some of Alma's own concerns about his son's eternal welfare. In chapter forty-one, Alma takes the opportunity to teach his son about the doctrine of personal restoration in that Corianton has "wrested the scriptures and gone far astray" (Alma 41:1) as it relates to the consequences that he may face for his sins. If Corianton had been indoctrinated with Satan's greatest weapon, which is evident, he would have at that time believed that there were no consequences to his actions and that "God will beat us with a few stripes, and at last we shall be saved in the kingdom of God" (2 Nephi 28:8). Alma's teachings to Corianton correcting this specific doctrine is central to his concerned instruction, and it is one of the priceless elements of the plain and precious gospel that the Book of Mormon makes available to us, since it is found nowhere else in scripture.

> I say unto thee, my son, that the plan of restoration is requisite with the justice of God; for it is requisite that all things should be restored to their proper order. Behold it is requisite and just, according to the power and resurrection of Christ, that the soul of man should be restored to its body, and that every part of the body should be restored to itself.
>
> And it is requisite with the justice of God that men should be judged according to their works; and if their works were good in this life, and the desires of their hearts were good, that they should also, at the last day, be restored unto that which is good.
>
> And if their works are evil they shall be restored unto them for evil. Therefore, all things shall be restored to their proper order, every thing to its natural frame. (Alma 41:2–4)

Alma teaches that this principle of personal restoration is "according to the power and resurrection of Christ," or in other words by the power of the Atonement and the natural consequence of the choices we make. If we have desired happiness, or good, we will be restored to happiness; if we have desired righteousness through our repentance, we shall be rewarded with righteousness. If we have desired evil, we "shall have [our] reward of evil when the night cometh" (Alma 41:5). He continues: "[Those who have repented, desired righteousness, and have been rewarded unto righteousness] are they that are redeemed of the Lord; yea, these are they that are taken out, that are delivered from that endless night of darkness; and thus they stand or fall; for behold, they are their own judges, whether to do good or do evil" (Alma 41:7).

In other words, those who are restored to righteousness are those whom the Savior's sacrifice redeems. They are their own judges. They have total, unfettered powers of agency. Alma says that this process and consequence is unalterable and reinforces our ability to exercise our agency to be redeemed: "whosoever will, may walk therein and be saved" (Alma 41:8).

We cannot expect God to turn away His all-seeing eye and to suspend eternal principles that govern the very organization of the heavens to have sin restored to happiness. To do so would be against the very nature of God. It would be contrary to the new and everlasting covenant into which God has entered. It would deny the Savior and deny the Atonement.

Alma declares: "Behold I say unto you, wickedness never was happiness" (Alma 41:10). "For behold, justice exerciseth all his demands, and also mercy claimeth all which is her own; and thus, none but the truly penitent are saved. What, do ye suppose that mercy can rob justice? I say unto you, Nay; not one whit. If so, God would cease to be God" (Alma 42:24–25).

If you or I or Corianton believe that in the Resurrection, when "even a hair of the head shall not be lost," that we will be restored to a state that is unnatural to us, we are mistaken. God will not—cannot—make us happy, good, or righteous against our will. We will be our own judge as to whom we have become, and our outcome cannot be otherwise. This is the point at which the principles of repentance, agency, atonement, and restoration all intersect.

> And now remember, remember, my brethren, that whosoever perisheth, perisheth unto himself; and whosoever doeth iniquity, doeth it unto himself; for behold ye are free; ye are permitted to act for yourselves; for behold, God hath given unto you a knowledge and he hath made you free.
>
> He hath given unto you that ye might know good from evil, and

he hath given unto you that ye might choose life or death; and ye can do good and be restored unto that which is good, or have that which is good restored unto you; or ye can do evil, and have that which is evil restored unto you. (Helaman 14:30–31)

O, my son, this is not the case; but the meaning of the word restoration is to bring back again evil for evil, or carnal for carnal, or devilish for devilish—good for that which is good; righteous for that which is righteous; just for that which is just; merciful for that which is merciful.

Therefore, my son, see that you are merciful unto your brethren; deal justly, judge righteously, and do good continually; and if ye do all these things then shall ye receive your reward; yea, ye shall have mercy restored unto you again; ye shall have justice restored unto you again; ye shall have a righteous judgment restored unto you again; and ye shall have good rewarded unto you again.

For that which ye do send out shall return unto you again, and be restored, therefore, the word restoration more fully condemneth the sinner, and justifieth him not at all. (Alma 41:13–15)

These verses help us to understand on another level the principle that as we forgive others, so will we be forgiven; and judge not unrighteously, lest we be judged. The golden rule, "whatsoever ye would that men should do to you, do ye even so to them" (Matthew 7:12), takes on a new meaning also. It is more than just a good idea for living; it is a simple truth with a complex meaning and eternally binding consequences.

When the time comes that all things are restored to their proper frame and are finally in their proper order following the tests of earth life, it will be the Lord and Savior, even Jesus the Christ, to whom we will turn in humble tears of gratitude for making the powers of the new and everlasting covenant—the Atonement—available to us.

We will then have a sure knowledge that it is only through His infinite, holy, and eternal sacrifice, fulfilled by sacred covenant, that our agency on earth was preserved, our repentance possible, our exaltation attainable, our forgiveness sure and our restoration made complete. The new and everlasting covenant, made possible by the Savior, will have been, for us, fulfilled.

Appendix

WHILE ON MY MISSION IN SINGAPORE, MY COMPANION and I were studying the twelfth chapter in Revelation, the first six verses. The first part of the chapter refers to the War in Heaven.

> And there appeared a great wonder in heaven; a woman clothed with the sun, and the moon under her feet, and upon her head a crown of twelve stars:
>
> And she being with child cried, travailing in birth, and pained to be delivered.
>
> And there appeared another wonder in heaven; and behold a great red dragon, having seven heads and ten horns, and seven crowns upon his heads.
>
> And his tail drew the third part of the stars of heaven, and did cast them to the earth: and the dragon stood before the woman which was ready to be delivered, for to devour her child as soon as it was born. (Revelation 12:1–4)

The dragon is symbolic of Satan. The "great wonder in heaven" refers to the War in Heaven, and the "third part of the stars of heaven" are those who chose to follow Lucifer. The child represents the Savior, whom Satan was prepared to devour in order to destroy God's plan.

"And she brought forth a man child, who was to rule all nations with a rod of iron: and her child was caught up unto God, and to his throne. And the woman fled into the wilderness, where she hath a place prepared of God, that they should feed her there a thousand two hundred and threescore days" (Revelation 12:5–6).

Jesus was born, served his foreordained purpose by providing atonement in fulfillment of the covenant He made in premortal life, and was received to a crown of glory. And the Church—described as "the woman" in the scripture (which is appropriate in the sense that the Church is the bride to the bridegroom of the Lord)—"fled into the wilderness" during a time of apostasy. My companion and I marveled at the fact that verse six appears to specify exactly how long the Apostasy was to last: 1,260 days. That's almost three and a half years. It didn't make sense.

This is where we began to speculate. Because of differences in calendars used by different cultures, we wondered if the 1,260 "days" referred to in verse six might not actually mean "years" instead. Our second speculation was that the years might not be calculated in terms of the solar calendar that we are accustomed to but instead may be figured using a lunar calendar. I am not a calendar expert by any means, so I don't know if this supposition makes any sense, but I seem to recall hearing that early cultures used the moon for tracking months and years. (To this day, I don't know much about the calendar that John used when he wrote this revelation.) Nevertheless, since this was just a theory anyway, what could it hurt to see where it goes?

Somewhere, we found out how long a lunar year actually was. Then, we calculated that 1,260 solar years equals 1,222.48 lunar years. If our theory was correct, the event that determined the start of the Apostasy could be identified by a time line and simple mathematics. We know that the Church of Jesus Christ was restored in AD 1830, signifying the end of the Apostasy. By subtracting 1,222.48 years from 1830, we arrived at an Apostasy starting date of about AD 607.75.

That was as far as we could go with our theory. Neither of us was familiar enough with world history to know anything that occurred within a very broad range of that specific date. So our theory sat for a while.

When I returned home from my mission, I worked in Reno, Nevada, while I took classes at the local community college and attended the Institute of Religion at the University of Nevada. One day, I decided to dust off this old idea that my companion and I had developed to see if I could put some specifics on our Apostasy starting date. I spent my free hours for more than a few days at the university library looking for a significant event that occurred in the middle of AD 607. Finally, I found something!

I was elated for only a brief second. My discovery was located in a dusty, old encyclopedia written in Italian. I could read the date but none of the text. However, I realized that I had more than one friend at the Institute who had served a mission in Italy. I rushed straight over to the Institute building, where I found one of my Italian-speaking returned-missionary friends, Robert Rudolfi. Anxiously, I drug Robert away from a ping-pong table—maybe it was the kitchen; I don't remember—and back to the library where he interpreted my discovery.

Here is what I found: In AD 607, Phocas, the emperor of Byzantine, issued the Pontificalis Notificalis. The decree issued an executive order mandating the people to recognize the Roman Pontiff as the supreme religious ruler and authority. Violators would suffer under penalty of death. This single event marked a temporary end of agency in the Church.

Suggested Reading

CHAPTER ONE

The Fruit of Repentance

Burton, Theodore M. "To Forgive Is Divine." *Ensign.* May 1983.

Edgley, Richard C. "The Empowerment of Humility." *Ensign.* Nov. 2003.

Hanks, Marion D. "Forgiveness: The Ultimate Form of Love." *Ensign.* Jan. 1974.

Jensen, Marlin K. "To Walk Humbly with Thy God." *Ensign.* May 2001.

Maxwell, Neal A. "According to the Desire of (Our) Hearts." *Ensign.* Nov. 1996.

———. "Testifying of the Great and Glorious Atonement." *Ensign.* Oct. 2001.

Oaks, Dallin H. "The Desires of Our Hearts." *Ensign.* June 1986.

Packer, Boyd K. "Personal Revelation: The Gift, the Test, and the Promise." *Ensign.* Nov. 1994.

CHAPTER TWO

Second Only to Faith

Kimball, Spencer W. *The Miracle of Forgiveness.* Salt Lake City: Bookcraft 1971.

Maxwell, Neal A. "Repentance." *Ensign.* Nov. 1991.

Eyring, Henry B. "Do Not Delay." *Ensign.* Nov. 1999.

Brockbank, Bernard P. "The Divine Power of Repentance." *Ensign.* Nov. 1974.

CHAPTER THREE

The Keys of Repentance

Oaks, Dallin H. "The Aaronic Priesthood and the Sacrament." *Ensign.* Nov. 1998.
McMullin, Keith B. "Behold the Man." *Ensign.* Nov. 1997.

CHAPTER FOUR

The New and Everlasting Covenant

Nelson, Russell M. "Children of the Covenant." *Ensign.* May 1995.
———. "The Atonement." *Ensign.* Nov 1996.
Romney, Marion G. "Gospel Covenants." *Ensign.* May 1981.
Burton, Theodore M. "Salvation and Exaltation." *Ensign.* July 1972.

CHAPTER FIVE

The Repentance Process

Neuenschwander, Dennis B. "The Path of Growth." *Ensign.* Dec. 1999.
Cullimore, James A. "Confession and Forsaking: Elements of Genuine Repentance." *Ensign.* Dec. 1971.
Hinckley, Gordon B. "And Peter Went Out and Wept Bitterly." *Ensign.* May 1979.
Clarke, J. Richard. "Confession." *New Era.* Nov. 1980.
Dunford, Robert R. and Jill W. "When 'I'm Sorry' Isn't Enough: Teaching the Principle of Restitution." *Ensign.* Oct. 1984.

CHAPTER SIX

Satan's Alternatives to Repentance

Oaks, Dallin H. "Be Not Deceived," *Ensign,* Nov. 2004.
Romney, Marion G. "Satan: The Great Deceiver," *Ensign,* June 1971.
Edgley, Richard C. "Satan's Bag of Snipes," *Ensign,* Nov. 2000.

CHAPTER SEVEN

Councils of Repentance

Ballard, M. Russell. "A Chance to Start Over: Church Disciplinary Councils and the Restoration of Blessings," *Ensign,* Sept. 1990.
Simpson, Robert L. "Courts of Love," *Ensign,* July 1972.
Hinckley, Gordon B. "The Stake President," *Ensign,* May 2000.

CHAPTER EIGHT

Man's Agency

Romney, Marion G. "The Perfect Law of Liberty." *Ensign.* Nov. 1981.
Stapley, Delbert L. "Using Our Free Agency." *Ensign.* May 1975.
Kendrick, L. Lionel "Our Moral Agency." *Ensign.* Mar. 1996.
Condie, Spencer J. "Agency: The Gift of Choices." *Ensign.* Sept. 1995.
Hunter, Howard W. "The Golden Thread of Choice." *Ensign.* Nov. 1989.
Packer, Boyd K. "Atonement, Agency, Accountability." *Ensign.* May 1988.

CHAPTER NINE

The Doctrine of the Restoration

Faust, James E. "He Restoreth My Soul." *Ensign.* Oct. 1997.

About the Author

When he was only ten years old, Derek G. Rowley moved to Carson City, Nevada, where the first person he met, Genine Kidder, became the love of his life and future eternal companion. Two weeks later, he announced to his parents at the dinner table that he had found the girl he was going to marry.

Derek served as a full-time missionary from 1982–84 in Singapore and Malaysia, where his love and testimony of the gospel of Jesus Christ became firm. Three years after returning from his mission, Derek married his best friend, Genine, in the Oakland Temple.

After attending Dixie College and the University of Nevada, he eventually left his studies to find his way in the business world. He worked for the Nevada Legislature and started Superior Capital Corporation, which would eventually become a family of companies that serves small businesses around the world. Derek is now the president and CEO of the corporation. He is the author of *The Nevada Corporation Handbook* and *Stupid Things Entrepreneurs Do to Ruin a Perfectly Good Business.*

Derek taught early-morning seminary for several years in Carson City and has served in many capacities in the Church, including high counselor and bishop.

Derek and his wife live in St. George, Utah, with their four sons.